I0021064

Mastering Go, The Complete Guide to Building Scalable Applications

Unlock the Power of Go Language for High-Performance Software Development

Booker Blunt

Rafael Sanders

Miguel Farmer

Boozman Richard

All rights reserved

No part of this book may be reproduced, distributed, or transmitted in any form or by any means without the prior written permission of the publisher, except in the case of brief quotations embodied in critical reviews and certain other noncommercial uses permitted by right law.

Contents

How to Scan a Barcode to Get a Repository

1. **Install a QR/Barcode Scanner** – Ensure you have a barcode or QR code scanner app installed on your smartphone or use a built-in scanner in **GitHub, GitLab, or Bitbucket.**

2. **Open the Scanner** – Launch the scanner app and grant necessary camera permissions.

3. **Scan the Barcode** – Align the barcode within the scanning frame. The scanner will automatically detect and process it.

4. **Follow the Link** – The scanned result will display a **URL to the repository.** Tap the link to open it in your web browser or Git client.

5. **Clone the Repository** – Use **Git clone** with the provided URL to download the repository to your local machine.

Chapter 1: Introduction to Go

1. Introduction

The landscape of programming languages is ever-evolving, with new tools emerging to meet the needs of modern software development. Among these, Go has distinguished itself as a language engineered for simplicity, efficiency, and robust performance. In this chapter, we begin our journey into the world of Go—a language designed with scalability and concurrency in mind.

Go's origins can be traced back to 2007, when a group of experienced engineers at Google set out to create a language that addressed the challenges of building large, distributed systems. Released as an open-source project in 2009, Go was built from the ground up with the philosophy of "less is more." Its creators wanted a language that could simplify the development process while still offering the power required to build high-performance applications.

Why Go Matters

In today's software landscape, applications must be both fast and capable of handling multiple tasks simultaneously. Traditional languages often require developers to wrestle with complex concurrency models or verbose syntax. Go, however, strikes a balance by providing native support for concurrency, ensuring that applications can scale without becoming overly complex. Its streamlined syntax and built-in garbage collection mean that developers can focus on writing clear, effective code rather than managing low-level details.

For instance, consider a scenario where a web service needs to handle thousands of concurrent requests. Languages that require manual thread management can bog down under this load. Go's goroutines—lightweight threads that are simple to use and highly efficient—make it easy to implement concurrent processing without sacrificing performance or clarity.

Who Should Read This Book

This guide is designed for a diverse audience:

- **Beginners:** Those new to programming will find that Go's simple syntax and clear structure make it an excellent introduction to modern software development.

- **Intermediate Programmers:** Developers with some experience can deepen their understanding of scalable architectures and concurrency patterns while learning best practices.

- **Professionals:** Experienced developers seeking to optimize performance and build high-performance, distributed systems will appreciate Go's advanced features.

- **Hobbyists:** Even those programming for fun will enjoy Go's practicality, as the language is versatile enough to tackle a wide range of projects—from web services to command-line tools.

Throughout this chapter, you will gain insight into why Go has become the go-to language for building scalable applications. We will explore its origins, core design principles, and the practical advantages it offers. By the end of this chapter, you should have a solid understanding of the foundations of Go and feel inspired to explore its capabilities further.

2. Core Concepts and Theory

To appreciate Go's design and its advantages for building scalable applications, it's important to delve into its core concepts and theoretical underpinnings. This section covers the history, philosophy, and key features that make Go unique.

A Brief History of Go

Go emerged from the practical needs of engineers working on large-scale systems at Google. The team wanted a language that could handle the complexity of modern software without the overhead and clumsiness of traditional languages. Go was created to reduce build times, simplify code maintenance, and enhance performance. Its development was influenced by a range of earlier languages—from C's efficiency to Python's readability—resulting in a language that marries the best attributes of its predecessors.

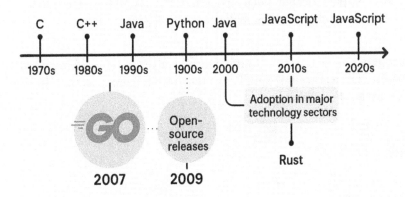

Go's Design Philosophy

At its core, Go follows a design philosophy centered on simplicity and clarity. Here are the key elements:

- **Minimalism:** Go's syntax is intentionally simple. This minimalism is not a limitation; rather, it is a tool to reduce cognitive load and potential bugs.

- **Concurrency as a First-Class Citizen:** Unlike many languages that treat concurrency as an afterthought, Go was built from the ground up with concurrency in mind. Its lightweight goroutines and channels allow developers to write concurrent code that is both clear and efficient.

- **Robust Performance:** Go compiles quickly to native code, ensuring high performance. Its efficient memory management via garbage collection and low-level system access means that performance is not sacrificed for simplicity.

- **Readability and Maintainability:** Code written in Go is easy to read and maintain. The language encourages a clear style that facilitates collaboration and long-term project maintenance.

Concurrency: The Heart of Scalability

One of the most revolutionary aspects of Go is its built-in support for concurrency. Unlike traditional multi-threaded programming—which can involve complex locking mechanisms and race conditions—Go offers goroutines and channels that make concurrent programming both safe and simple.

Goroutines allow functions to run concurrently with minimal overhead. You can start a goroutine simply by prefixing a function call with the keyword go. For example:

```go
package main

import (
    "fmt"
    "time"
)

func greet(name string) {
    fmt.Printf("Hello, %s!\n", name)
}

func main() {
    go greet("Alice")
    time.Sleep(100 * time.Millisecond) // Allow
goroutine to finish
}
```

In this snippet, the greet function runs concurrently as a goroutine. The use of a short sleep ensures that the main function does not exit before the goroutine has a chance to print its output.

Channels provide a means for goroutines to communicate. They allow you to send and receive values safely across concurrent processes. Consider the following example:

```go
```

```
package main

import "fmt"

func sum(a []int, result chan int) {
    total := 0
    for _, value := range a {
        total += value
    }
    result <- total  // Send result back through the
channel
}

func main() {
    numbers := []int{1, 2, 3, 4, 5}
    result := make(chan int)
    go sum(numbers, result)
    fmt.Println("Sum:", <-result)
}
```

This code demonstrates how a channel facilitates safe communication between the main routine and a goroutine computing a sum.

Simplicity and Performance

Go's simplicity is by design. Every feature of the language has been carefully considered to balance ease of use with high performance. Developers appreciate that Go avoids overly complex abstractions while still offering the tools necessary to build powerful, efficient software. The language's garbage collector handles memory management automatically, letting developers focus on solving business problems rather than worrying about low-level memory allocation.

Furthermore, Go's compilation to native code provides a performance edge over interpreted languages. It offers near-C performance in many scenarios while retaining a much higher level of abstraction and ease of use.

Real-World Analogies

Think of Go as a well-designed toolset for a craftsman. Just as a carpenter values a reliable set of tools that are simple yet effective, a developer values a language that lets them quickly build and maintain high-quality software. Go's clear syntax is like a finely honed saw—powerful in capable hands but easy enough for beginners to handle. Its concurrency features are akin to having multiple skilled assistants who can work in parallel without stepping on each other's toes.

Advantages for Scalable Applications

Scalability isn't just about handling increased load; it's about designing systems that can grow and adapt over time. Go's support for concurrency, its performance efficiency, and its straightforward syntax make it ideal for building applications that can scale from small projects to enterprise-level systems. Whether you're designing a microservice architecture for a large web application or building a lightweight command-line tool, Go's design principles help ensure that your code remains efficient, maintainable, and robust.

In summary, the core concepts and theory behind Go demonstrate that it is more than just another programming language—it is a thoughtfully engineered tool designed to simplify complex, high-performance computing tasks. Whether you are a novice learning the basics or a seasoned professional looking to optimize your systems, understanding these principles is crucial to leveraging the full power of Go.

3. Tools and Setup

Before diving into hands-on projects with Go, it's essential to set up your development environment. This section guides you through the necessary tools and step-by-step instructions to get started.

Required Tools and Platforms

To begin programming in Go, you'll need the following:

- **Go Compiler and Runtime:** Download the latest version of Go from the official Go website. This package includes the compiler, runtime, and tools necessary to build and run Go programs.

- **Integrated Development Environment (IDE):** While you can use any text editor, IDEs like Visual Studio Code, GoLand, or even Sublime Text with Go plugins offer enhanced support with syntax highlighting, code completion, and debugging tools.

- **Version Control:** Git is widely used for managing code changes. Installing Git helps you collaborate and track your project's evolution.

- **Terminal/Command Line Interface:** Familiarity with a terminal is crucial. Whether you're on Windows, macOS, or Linux, ensure you have access to a command line for executing Go commands.

Step-by-Step Environment Setup

1. Installing Go

- **Download:**
  Visit the official Go downloads page and choose the installer that corresponds to your operating system.

- **Installation:**
  Run the installer and follow the on-screen instructions. By default, Go is installed in a directory such as /usr/local/go on Unix systems or C:\Go on Windows.

- **Verify Installation:**
  Open your terminal and run:

```bash
go version
```
You should see an output similar to:

```php-template
go version go1.XX.X <platform>/<architecture>
```
This confirms that Go is correctly installed.

2. Configuring Your Workspace

Go uses a workspace structure to organize code. The workspace typically includes three main directories:

- **src:** Contains your source code.

- **pkg:** Holds package objects.

- **bin:** Stores compiled executable binaries.

For example, on a Unix-like system, you might create a workspace like this:

bash

```
mkdir -p $HOME/go/{src,pkg,bin}
```
Then, set the GOPATH environment variable to point to this workspace:

bash

```
export GOPATH=$HOME/go
```
Add the Go binary path to your system's PATH so you can run Go commands from any location:

bash

```
export PATH=$PATH:$GOPATH/bin
```

3. Choosing an IDE

While you can start with any text editor, Visual Studio Code (VS Code) is a popular choice. To set up VS Code for Go development:

- **Install VS Code:** Download and install from Visual Studio Code's website.

- **Install the Go Extension:** Launch VS Code and go to the Extensions tab. Search for "Go" and install the official extension by the Go team.

- **Configure the Extension:** The extension may prompt you to install additional tools (such as gopls for language support and debugging tools). Follow the on-screen instructions to complete the setup.

4. Additional Tools

- **Git:**
  Install Git from git-scm.com if you haven't already. Configure it with your user details:

bash

```
git config --global user.name "Your Name"
git config --global user.email
"youremail@example.com"
```

- **Debugger:**
  The Go extension in VS Code comes with integrated debugging support. Learn the basics of setting breakpoints and inspecting variables by reviewing the extension's documentation.

By the end of this setup process, you will have a fully functional Go development environment. You're now ready to write, build, and run your first Go programs.

4. Hands-on Examples & Projects

The best way to master Go is by diving into real projects. This section guides you through several hands-on examples that illustrate core concepts while reinforcing best practices.

Project 1: Hello, Go! – Your First Program

Begin with a simple "Hello, World!" program. Create a file named hello.go with the following code:

```go
package main

import "fmt"

// main is the entry point of the program.
func main() {
    fmt.Println("Hello, Go!")
}
```

Walkthrough:

- **Code Structure:**
  The package main declaration tells Go that this file is an executable package.

- **Importing Libraries:**
  The fmt package provides formatting for input and output.

- **Function:**
  The main() function is the entry point. It calls fmt.Println to print the greeting.

Compile and run this program using:

```bash
```

```
go run hello.go
```
Visual Aid:
A simple flowchart can depict the program's execution: Start → main() → Print to console → End.

Project 2: A Simple Command-Line Tool

Next, build a basic command-line interface (CLI) tool that accepts user input and performs a simple calculation. Create a file named calculator.go:

```go

package main

import (
    "fmt"
    "os"
    "strconv"
)

// add returns the sum of two integers.
func add(a, b int) int {
    return a + b
}

func main() {
    if len(os.Args) < 3 {
        fmt.Println("Usage: calculator <num1> <num2>")
        return
    }
    num1, err1 := strconv.Atoi(os.Args[1])
    num2, err2 := strconv.Atoi(os.Args[2])
    if err1 != nil || err2 != nil {
        fmt.Println("Please enter valid integers.")
        return
    }
    fmt.Printf("The sum of %d and %d is %d\n", num1, num2, add(num1, num2))
}
```

Walkthrough:

- **Command-Line Arguments:**
  The program uses os.Args to read input from the command line.

- **Conversion and Validation:**
  strconv.Atoi converts string arguments to integers, with error checking.

- **Calculation:**
  The add function computes the sum and prints the result.

Run this tool from the terminal:

```bash
go run calculator.go 10 20
```

Project 3: Building a Simple Web Server

Go's strength in concurrency makes it ideal for web applications. In this project, you'll build a basic web server. Create a file named server.go:

```go
package main

import (
    "fmt"
    "net/http"
)

// homeHandler handles requests to the root URL.
func homeHandler(w http.ResponseWriter, r
*http.Request) {
    fmt.Fprintf(w, "Welcome to the Go Web Server!")
}

func main() {
    http.HandleFunc("/", homeHandler)
    fmt.Println("Server starting at :8080")
    err := http.ListenAndServe(":8080", nil)
    if err != nil {
        fmt.Println("Error starting server:", err)
    }
```

```
}
```
Walkthrough:

- **HTTP Package:**
  The built-in net/http package provides all the tools needed to create a web server.

- **Handler Function:**
  homeHandler is defined to handle HTTP requests and send a welcome message.

- **Starting the Server:**
  The server listens on port 8080 and routes incoming requests to homeHandler.

Test the server by navigating to http://localhost:8080 in your web browser.

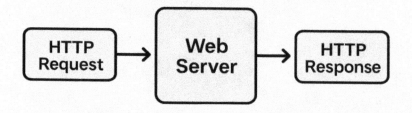

Project 4: Developing a Microservice

For a more advanced hands-on example, consider building a microservice. This project will introduce you to RESTful API design using Go. Create a new file called microservice.go:

```go
package main
```

```
import (
    "encoding/json"
    "log"
    "net/http"
)

// User represents a user object in our microservice.
type User struct {
    ID     int     `json:"id"`
    Name   string  `json:"name"`
}

// In-memory user data.
var users = []User{
    {ID: 1, Name: "Alice"},
    {ID: 2, Name: "Bob"},
}

// getUsers handles GET requests and returns a list
of users.
func getUsers(w http.ResponseWriter, r *http.Request)
{
    w.Header().Set("Content-Type",
"application/json")
    json.NewEncoder(w).Encode(users)
}

func main() {
    http.HandleFunc("/users", getUsers)
    log.Println("Microservice running on port 8080")
    log.Fatal(http.ListenAndServe(":8080", nil))
}
```

Walkthrough:

- **RESTful API:**
  The endpoint /users returns a JSON-encoded list of user objects.

- **JSON Handling:**
  The encoding/json package is used to convert Go structs to JSON.

- **Logging and Error Handling:**
  The built-in log package provides logging to help diagnose issues during development.

Run the microservice using:

bash

```
go run microservice.go
```
Then, use a tool like curl or Postman to send a GET request to:

bash

```
curl http://localhost:8080/users
```
The response will be a JSON array of user objects.

Wrapping Up the Projects

These projects are designed to build upon one another. Starting with simple programs like "Hello, Go!" and progressing to more complex applications such as a web server and microservice, you will gain hands-on experience with the core aspects of Go. Each project reinforces fundamental concepts such as:

- Clean code structure and organization

- Effective use of built-in libraries

- Basic concurrency with goroutines and channels

- Real-world application of RESTful API design

Throughout these examples, note the emphasis on readability and maintainability. Code comments and logical flow are key components in building scalable software. The projects also demonstrate that, with Go, you can quickly prototype and deploy applications—from command-line tools to web services—making it an ideal language for both learning and professional development.

---

5. Advanced Techniques & Optimization

As you gain confidence with Go, exploring advanced techniques can help you fine-tune your applications for even greater performance and scalability. In this section, we discuss strategies for optimization and best practices for handling complex, concurrent systems.

Performance Tuning

Optimizing Go applications involves a careful balance between clarity and efficiency. Profiling tools such as Go's built-in pprof package can help identify bottlenecks. For example, adding a simple profiling setup in your code can pinpoint functions that consume excessive CPU time or memory. Consider this snippet:

```go
import (
    "net/http"
    _ "net/http/pprof"
)

func main() {
    go func() {

log.Println(http.ListenAndServe("localhost:6060",
nil))
    }()
    // Application code here
}
```

Accessing http://localhost:6060/debug/pprof/ in your browser provides a visual report of your application's performance.

Advanced Concurrency Patterns

Beyond basic goroutines and channels, Go supports complex concurrency patterns such as worker pools, fan-out/fan-in, and pipelining. These techniques can distribute tasks efficiently across multiple cores. For instance, a worker pool pattern allows you to control the number of concurrent tasks:

```go
func worker(id int, jobs <-chan int, results chan<-
int) {
    for j := range jobs {
        fmt.Printf("Worker %d processing job %d\n",
id, j)
        results <- j * 2  // Simulated work
    }
}
```

Using multiple workers ensures that your application handles large workloads gracefully, while channels manage data flow seamlessly.

Best Practices

- **Code Readability:**
  Maintain clear and consistent coding styles to simplify maintenance.

- **Error Handling:**
  Always check and handle errors explicitly to avoid subtle bugs.

- **Documentation:**
  Write inline documentation and use tools like GoDoc to generate readable API references.

- **Testing:**
  Implement comprehensive testing strategies using Go's testing framework to ensure code reliability under concurrent loads.

---

6. Troubleshooting and Problem-Solving

Even the best-designed systems encounter issues. This section outlines common pitfalls and offers practical troubleshooting tips.

Common Challenges

1. **Race Conditions:**
   When multiple goroutines access shared resources without proper synchronization, unpredictable behavior can occur. Use Go's -race flag during testing to detect these issues.

2. **Memory Leaks:**
   Although Go manages memory automatically, improper use of slices or unclosed resources can lead to leaks. Profiling tools and careful code review help mitigate this risk.

3. **Dependency Management:**
   As projects grow, managing external packages can become

challenging. The use of Go modules simplifies dependency tracking and version control.

Debugging Techniques

- **Verbose Logging:**
  Use logging judiciously to trace the execution of your program. Tools like log.Printf can provide insights into code paths and variable values.

- **Unit Testing:**
  Write tests for individual functions to isolate and identify bugs quickly. The built-in testing package is simple and powerful.

- **Code Reviews:**
  Collaborate with peers to review code. Fresh eyes often catch issues that may have been overlooked.

Before-and-After Example:
Consider a scenario where a race condition is causing sporadic failures. By adding a mutex lock to synchronize access, you can transform unreliable behavior into a stable system. Compare code before and after to understand the change.

---

7. Conclusion & Next Steps

In this chapter, we have laid the foundation for understanding Go as a language built for modern, scalable applications. We began by exploring its history and design philosophy, highlighting the simplicity and power of its core features. Through practical examples—from the classic "Hello, World!" to building a microservice—we demonstrated how Go's straightforward syntax and robust concurrency model make it a compelling choice for developers at all levels.

Key Takeaways

- **Go's Origins and Philosophy:**
  The language was designed with simplicity, efficiency, and scalability in mind, offering a minimalist syntax combined with powerful concurrency features.

- **Concurrency as a Core Strength:**
  Goroutines and channels provide an intuitive model for
  concurrent programming, making it easy to build responsive, high-
  performance systems.

- **Hands-on Practice:**
  Through a series of practical projects, you've seen how to create
  command-line tools, web servers, and RESTful APIs, setting the
  stage for more advanced work.

- **Advanced Techniques:**
  Optimization strategies and advanced concurrency patterns ensure
  that your applications not only function correctly but also perform
  efficiently at scale.

- **Problem-Solving Strategies:**
  Common pitfalls such as race conditions and memory leaks can
  be addressed with proper testing, debugging, and adherence to
  best practices.

Next Steps

Now that you have a comprehensive introduction to Go, the next chapters
will build on these foundations. Expect to dive deeper into more complex
topics like microservices architecture, advanced debugging techniques, and
performance tuning in high-load environments. Additional resources—
including online communities, documentation, and further reading—will
be provided to help you continue your journey.

As you progress, remember that programming is both a craft and an art.
Experiment with the code, explore different design patterns, and don't
hesitate to innovate. The hands-on projects in this book are just the
beginning—each challenge is an opportunity to refine your skills and build
systems that are not only scalable but also maintainable and robust.

With this solid grounding in the fundamentals, you are now ready to
embrace the full potential of Go. Let this chapter serve as the springboard
for your future projects, where the principles of simplicity, concurrency,
and performance will guide you in building truly scalable applications.

Chapter 2: Getting Started with Go

In this chapter, you will embark on your journey with Go by setting up your development environment, writing your first program, and learning the foundational concepts of the language. Whether you're a beginner exploring programming for the first time, a professional aiming to pick up a new language, or a hobbyist ready to experiment with a modern, efficient tool, this chapter will provide you with the essential knowledge and hands-on projects to get started.

---

1. Introduction

Go, also known as Golang, is celebrated for its simplicity, speed, and built-in support for concurrency. In today's fast-paced world of software development, building applications that are both efficient and scalable is crucial. Go was designed with these requirements in mind, making it a top choice for developing everything from small command-line tools to large-scale distributed systems.

Why This Chapter Matters

As you begin your journey with Go, the first step is to create a solid foundation. This chapter covers:

- **Setting Up Your Environment:** Learn how to install Go, configure your workspace, and select an IDE that fits your workflow.

- **Writing Your First Program:** Explore the "Hello World" example to get acquainted with Go's syntax and structure.

- **Understanding Basic Concepts:** Grasp core ideas like variables, data types, functions, and control structures that will serve as building blocks for more advanced topics.

This chapter is not just a walkthrough—it is a comprehensive guide designed to empower you with the skills needed to dive into Go development confidently. You will encounter step-by-step instructions, detailed code examples, and practical analogies that connect abstract ideas to real-world applications.

Key Terminology

Before we dive in, let's clarify some key terms:

- **Compiler:** A tool that converts your source code into machine code.

- **Workspace:** The directory structure where your Go code and packages are organized.

- **IDE (Integrated Development Environment):** A software application that provides tools for writing, testing, and debugging code.

- **Syntax:** The set of rules that define the combinations of symbols that are considered to be correctly structured programs in a language.

- **Control Structures:** Constructs that control the flow of execution in a program, such as loops and conditional statements.

Setting the Tone

This chapter is designed to be engaging and accessible. You will find that complex ideas are broken down into manageable pieces with plenty of real-world examples. The narrative is professional and approachable, ensuring that whether you're coding for work or leisure, you feel confident as you step through each concept. With a blend of theory, practical steps, and clear explanations, this chapter lays the groundwork for your journey into Go programming.

---

2. Core Concepts and Theory

To build a solid understanding of Go, it is essential to learn its core concepts. In this section, we delve into the fundamental building blocks of the language: variables, data types, functions, and control structures. Each concept is explained in depth, using real-world analogies and practical examples.

Variables and Data Types

What Are Variables?

Variables are storage containers for data that can change during program execution. Think of them as labeled jars where you can store ingredients. In Go, variables have a specific type, such as integer, string, or boolean, which dictates what kind of data can be stored in them.

Example:

```go
package main

import "fmt"

func main() {
    var greeting string = "Hello, Go!"
    fmt.Println(greeting)
}
```

In this example, the variable greeting is declared as a string and initialized with a message. The fmt.Println function is then used to output the value.

Real-World Analogy:
Imagine you're organizing a toolbox. Each tool (variable) is stored in a compartment (type) that is designed for it. A wrench (integer) will not fit in the compartment for screwdrivers (strings).

Data Types in Go

Go has a robust type system that includes:

- **Basic Types:**
    - **Integers:** int, int8, int16, etc.
    - **Floating-Point Numbers:** float32, float64
    - **Boolean:** bool
    - **String:** A sequence of characters
- **Composite Types:**
    - **Arrays:** Fixed-size sequences of elements.

- ○ **Slices:** Dynamically-sized arrays.

- ○ **Maps:** Collections of key-value pairs.

- ○ **Structs:** Custom composite types that group related values.

Each type comes with its own set of operations and functions. Understanding data types is crucial because they affect how you manipulate and store data in your applications.

DATA TYPES

Type	Example
int	42
string	"Hello"
bool	true

Functions and Their Role

What Is a Function?

A function in Go is a block of code designed to perform a specific task. Functions help you break down complex tasks into manageable pieces, making your code more modular and easier to maintain.

Example:

```go
package main
```

```
import "fmt"

// add returns the sum of two integers.
func add(a int, b int) int {
    return a + b
}

func main() {
    result := add(10, 5)
    fmt.Println("Result:", result)
}
```

This code defines an add function that takes two integers as parameters and returns their sum. Functions allow you to reuse code without rewriting it every time you need to perform the same operation.

Analogy:
Think of a function like a recipe in a cookbook. Once you know the recipe, you can prepare the dish (perform the task) repeatedly with different ingredients (parameters).

Function Syntax and Best Practices

- **Declaration:**
  Use the func keyword to declare functions.

- **Parameters and Return Types:**
  Clearly specify parameter types and the return type.

- **Documentation:**
  Comment your functions so that others (and your future self) understand their purpose.

Tip:
Consistent naming conventions and clear, concise comments go a long way in making your code understandable.

Control Structures: Directing Program Flow

Conditional Statements

Conditional statements allow your program to execute different code blocks based on certain conditions.

Example:

```go
go

package main

import "fmt"

func main() {
    age := 20
    if age >= 18 {
        fmt.Println("You are an adult.")
    } else {
        fmt.Println("You are a minor.")
    }
}
```

Here, an if-else statement checks whether the variable age meets a condition and outputs a corresponding message.

Real-World Analogy:
Conditional statements are like traffic signals. They decide whether to stop, go, or yield based on the current situation.

Loops

Loops allow you to execute a block of code multiple times.

Example:

```go
go

package main

import "fmt"

func main() {
    for i := 1; i <= 5; i++ {
        fmt.Println("Iteration:", i)
    }
}
```

This for loop prints the iteration number five times. Go uses a single loop construct (for), which can be adapted to behave like a while-loop or a traditional counted loop.

Analogy:
Imagine a clock that ticks every second. Each tick represents one iteration of a loop until a condition (like reaching a specified number) is met.

Switch Statements

Switch statements offer a cleaner alternative to multiple if-else conditions.

Example:

```go
package main

import "fmt"

func main() {
    day := "Monday"
    switch day {
    case "Monday":
        fmt.Println("Start of the work week.")
    case "Friday":
        fmt.Println("End of the work week.")
    default:
        fmt.Println("Midweek days are busy.")
    }
}
```

Switch statements simplify decision-making in your code by comparing a variable against multiple values and executing the corresponding code block.

Bringing It All Together

In summary, core concepts in Go—variables, data types, functions, and control structures—form the backbone of every application you write. These components not only help you write concise and effective code but also encourage best practices like modularity and clarity.

Case Study:
Consider a simple banking application where you need to process transactions. Variables store account balances, functions handle deposit and withdrawal operations, and control structures determine if transactions are valid. By mastering these concepts, you gain the tools to solve real-world problems efficiently.

3. Tools and Setup

Before writing any code, you need a robust environment to develop, test, and debug your Go programs. This section provides step-by-step guidance on installing Go, configuring your workspace, and choosing an IDE.

Installing Go

Step 1: Downloading Go

- **Visit the Official Website:**
  Navigate to the Go Downloads page. Choose the installer for your operating system—Windows, macOS, or Linux.

- **Installation Process:**
  Run the installer and follow the on-screen instructions. On most systems, Go is installed in a default directory (for example, /usr/local/go on Unix-based systems or C:\Go on Windows).

Step 2: Verifying Installation

After installation, open a terminal or command prompt and type:

```bash
```

```
go version
```
A typical output might be:

```php-template
```

```
go version go1.XX.X <platform>/<architecture>
```
This confirms that Go is installed correctly and ready to use.

Configuring Your Workspace

Go uses a workspace—a specific directory structure—to organize code and dependencies.

Workspace Structure

Create a workspace with the following directories:

- **src:** Contains your source code.

- **pkg:** Stores package objects.

- **bin:** Holds compiled executable binaries.

Example:

```bash
```

```bash
mkdir -p $HOME/go/{src,pkg,bin}
```
Next, set the GOPATH environment variable to point to your workspace. Add the following lines to your shell configuration file (e.g., .bashrc or .zshrc):

```bash
```

```bash
export GOPATH=$HOME/go
export PATH=$PATH:$GOPATH/bin
```
Reload your configuration:

```bash
```

```bash
source ~/.bashrc
```

Choosing an IDE

While you can use any text editor, an Integrated Development Environment (IDE) enhances your productivity with features like code completion, syntax highlighting, and debugging tools.

Recommended IDEs

- **Visual Studio Code (VS Code):**
  A lightweight, popular IDE with a robust extension ecosystem.

- **GoLand:**
  A feature-rich, dedicated Go IDE.

- **Sublime Text:**
  A fast, minimalist editor with Go plugins.

Setting Up VS Code for Go:

1. Download and install Visual Studio Code.

2. Launch VS Code and open the Extensions pane.

3. Search for "Go" and install the official Go extension.

4. Follow prompts to install additional Go tools (e.g., gopls for language support).

Additional Tools

- **Version Control:**
  Install Git from git-scm.com. Configure it with your user details:

bash

```
git config --global user.name "Your Name"
git config --global user.email "you@example.com"
```

- **Terminal/Command Line:**
  Familiarize yourself with basic terminal commands. A reliable terminal is essential for running Go commands and scripts.

By the end of this section, you should have a fully configured Go development environment that supports your coding, testing, and debugging efforts.

---

4. Hands-on Examples & Projects

Now that your environment is set up and you understand the foundational concepts, it's time to put theory into practice. This section guides you through several projects that build on each other, starting with the classic "Hello World" and moving into more complex examples that reinforce your understanding of variables, functions, and control structures.

Project 1: Your First Program – Hello, Go!

Step-by-Step Walkthrough

1. **Create a File:**
   Open your IDE and create a file named hello.go in your workspace's src directory.

2. **Write the Code:**
   Insert the following code:

go

```
package main

import "fmt"

// main is the entry point for the program.
func main() {
    fmt.Println("Hello, Go!")
}
```

3. **Compile and Run:**
   Open your terminal, navigate to the file's directory, and run:

```bash
go run hello.go
You should see the output:

Hello, Go!
```

Project 2: Exploring Variables and Data Types

Creating a Program to Demonstrate Variables

1. **Create a File:**
   Name it variables.go.

2. **Write the Code:**

```go
package main

import "fmt"

func main() {
    // Declare variables with explicit type
    var name string = "Go Developer"
    var age int = 30
    var active bool = true

    // Short variable declaration (type inferred)
    salary := 55000.50

    // Output variables
    fmt.Printf("Name: %s\nAge: %d\nActive:
%t\nSalary: %.2f\n", name, age, active, salary)
```

```
}
```

3. **Run and Observe:**
   Execute the program using:

```bash
bash
```

```
go run variables.go
```
Expected Output:
A formatted printout of each variable's value.

Real-World Application:
Consider this code as part of a simple user profile system where each variable holds information about a user. This practical example demonstrates how you can manage different data types within a single program.

Project 3: Functions and Modular Code
Building a Simple Calculator

Functions are essential for breaking down tasks. In this project, you will create a program that performs basic arithmetic operations.

1. **Create a File:**
   Name it calculator.go.

2. **Write the Code:**

```go
go

package main

import (
    "fmt"
    "os"
    "strconv"
)

// add returns the sum of two integers.
func add(a int, b int) int {
    return a + b
}

// subtract returns the difference between two
integers.
```

```
func subtract(a int, b int) int {
    return a - b
}

// main is the entry point of the program.
func main() {
    // Check if sufficient arguments are provided.
    if len(os.Args) < 4 {
        fmt.Println("Usage: calculator <operation> <num1> <num2>")
        fmt.Println("Operations: add, subtract")
        return
    }

    operation := os.Args[1]
    num1, err1 := strconv.Atoi(os.Args[2])
    num2, err2 := strconv.Atoi(os.Args[3])
    if err1 != nil || err2 != nil {
        fmt.Println("Invalid numbers provided.")
        return
    }

    switch operation {
    case "add":
        fmt.Printf("Result: %d\n", add(num1, num2))
    case "subtract":
        fmt.Printf("Result: %d\n", subtract(num1, num2))
    default:
        fmt.Println("Unsupported operation. Use add or subtract.")
    }
}
```

3. **Testing the Program:**
   Run the program from the terminal:

```bash
go run calculator.go add 15 10
```
and
```bash
go run calculator.go subtract 15 10
```

Project 4: Control Structures in Action

Creating a Program to Demonstrate Conditional Logic and Loops

1. **Create a File:**
   Name it control.go.

2. **Write the Code:**

```go
package main

import "fmt"

func main() {
    // Conditional logic
    temperature := 72
    if temperature > 75 {
        fmt.Println("It is warm outside.")
    } else if temperature < 65 {
        fmt.Println("It is cool outside.")
    } else {
        fmt.Println("The temperature is just right.")
    }

    // Loop: Print numbers 1 through 5
    fmt.Println("Counting from 1 to 5:")
    for i := 1; i <= 5; i++ {
        fmt.Println(i)
    }

    // Switch statement example
    day := "Saturday"
    switch day {
    case "Saturday", "Sunday":
        fmt.Println("It's the weekend!")
    default:
        fmt.Println("It's a weekday.")
    }
}
```

3. **Run and Verify:**
   Execute the program to observe different outputs based on conditions and loops.

Real-World Application:
Imagine this code being part of a weather monitoring system where conditions change based on sensor readings and time schedules.

Project 5: Combining Concepts into a Mini Application

Developing a Simple Command-Line To-Do List

This project ties together variables, functions, and control structures to create a mini application—a simple to-do list manager.

1. **Create a File:**
   Name it todo.go.

2. **Write the Code:**

```go
package main

import (
    "bufio"
    "fmt"
    "os"
    "strings"
)

// A slice to store tasks.
var tasks []string

// addTask appends a new task to the list.
func addTask(task string) {
    tasks = append(tasks, task)
    fmt.Println("Task added:", task)
}

// listTasks prints all tasks.
func listTasks() {
    fmt.Println("\nCurrent Tasks:")
    for index, task := range tasks {
        fmt.Printf("%d. %s\n", index+1, task)
    }
}
```

```go
func main() {
    reader := bufio.NewReader(os.Stdin)
    for {
        fmt.Println("\nChoose an option: add, list, or exit")
        input, _ := reader.ReadString('\n')
        input = strings.TrimSpace(input)

        switch input {
        case "add":
            fmt.Print("Enter task: ")
            task, _ := reader.ReadString('\n')
            addTask(strings.TrimSpace(task))
        case "list":
            listTasks()
        case "exit":
            fmt.Println("Exiting the application. Goodbye!")
            return
        default:
            fmt.Println("Invalid option. Please try again.")
        }
    }
}
```

3. **Running the To-Do List:**
   Execute with:

```bash
go run todo.go
```
Follow the interactive prompts to add and list tasks.

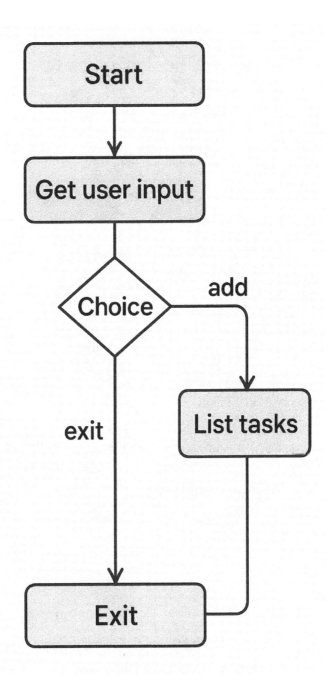

5. Advanced Techniques & Optimization

As you grow more comfortable with the basics, learning advanced techniques will help you write cleaner, more efficient code. In this section, we explore ways to optimize your code and introduce best practices that set the stage for scalable development.

Code Organization and Modularity

Organizing your code into packages and modules not only improves readability but also facilitates reuse. In Go, each file belongs to a package. Splitting functionality into distinct packages helps maintain a clear separation of concerns.

Example:
Imagine refactoring the to-do list application by moving task-related functions into their own package (tasks). This modular design makes testing and maintaining the code much simpler.

Optimization Tips

Memory Management

Go's garbage collector automatically manages memory, but you can still optimize performance by reducing allocations. Use slices efficiently, preallocate when possible, and avoid creating unnecessary objects in loops.

Concurrency and Parallelism

Even though this chapter focuses on getting started, understanding the basics of Go's concurrency can guide you as you write more complex applications. Use goroutines and channels carefully to avoid race conditions and ensure thread safety.

Tip:
Profile your applications with Go's pprof tool to identify bottlenecks.

Code Readability and Documentation

Clean code is easier to optimize. Use consistent naming conventions, comment your functions, and structure your code logically. Tools like

GoDoc can help generate documentation automatically from your comments.

Visual Aid Suggestion:
A flowchart comparing a monolithic function to a modular, well-organized codebase emphasizes the importance of refactoring for performance and maintainability.

Advanced Code Snippets

Below is an example of optimizing a function that processes a large slice of data by preallocating the result slice:

go

```go
func processData(data []int) []int {
    // Preallocate a slice for results
    results := make([]int, 0, len(data))
    for _, value := range data {
        // Simulate processing on each value
        results = append(results, value*2)
    }
    return results
}
```

Explanation:
By preallocating the slice with a capacity equal to the input data length, you avoid multiple memory reallocations during the append operations.

---

6. Troubleshooting and Problem-Solving

Learning to code is as much about problem-solving as it is about writing code. In this section, we cover common challenges you might encounter when starting with Go and provide practical advice on how to overcome them.

Common Issues

Environment Setup Challenges

- **Installation Errors:**
  If the go version command does not output the expected version, double-check your installation path and environment variables.

- **Workspace Configuration:**
  Problems with package imports often arise from incorrect GOPATH settings. Ensure your workspace is set up as described and that your IDE is configured to use it.

Code Errors and Debugging

- **Syntax Errors:**
  Go's compiler is strict about syntax. Missing a closing brace or semicolon can cause errors. Use your IDE's built-in error checking to catch these early.

- **Runtime Errors:**
  When dealing with command-line input or file operations, always check for errors returned by functions such as strconv.Atoi or file operations.

Before-and-After Example:
Consider a situation where a program crashes due to an unchecked error. By adding error handling:

```go
num, err := strconv.Atoi(os.Args[1])
if err != nil {
    fmt.Println("Error: Please provide a valid
number.")
    return
}
```

You improve the program's robustness and user experience.

Debugging Tools

- **Verbose Logging:**
  Use fmt.Printf or the log package to output variable values and program states.

- **Go's Race Detector:**
  When experimenting with concurrency, run your program with the -race flag to detect potential race conditions:

```bash
bash

go run -race yourprogram.go
```
Visual Aid Suggestion:
A screenshot of terminal output with the -race flag enabled can illustrate how potential issues are flagged during testing.

Best Practices for Troubleshooting

1. **Start Small:**
   Break down your code into small, testable units. Debug one function at a time.

2. **Use Version Control:**
   Commit your changes frequently. This way, you can easily roll back to a working version when encountering issues.

3. **Peer Reviews:**
   Sometimes another set of eyes can spot errors you've missed. Collaborate with peers or participate in online communities.

---

7. Conclusion & Next Steps

In this chapter, you have taken your first steps into the world of Go. We started by setting up your environment and quickly moved into writing your first "Hello World" program. Along the way, you learned about variables, data types, functions, and control structures—the foundational elements that will serve you well as you progress further.

Key Takeaways

- **Environment Setup:**
  A properly configured workspace and a supportive IDE are essential to a smooth development experience.

- **Hello World and Beyond:**
  Writing your first program is just the beginning. Experimenting with basic examples helps build confidence.

- **Core Concepts:**
  Understanding variables, data types, functions, and control

structures lays a solid foundation for more complex programming challenges.

- **Hands-On Practice:**
  The projects and examples provided in this chapter are designed to reinforce your learning by applying concepts in real-world scenarios.

- **Problem-Solving:**
  Embrace debugging and troubleshooting as integral parts of the coding process. Learning to identify and fix issues early will save you time and frustration later.

Next Steps

Now that you have a grasp on the basics of Go, the following chapters will build on these concepts. You will explore more advanced topics such as Go's powerful concurrency model, effective error handling, and strategies for developing scalable applications. Consider revisiting the projects in this chapter to experiment with additional features or to extend their functionality. For example, you might add new commands to your to-do list application or optimize the calculator to handle more operations.

Final Thoughts

Getting started with any new programming language can be challenging, but the simplicity and clarity of Go make it an excellent choice for both beginners and seasoned professionals. With the foundation you've built in this chapter, you are well-equipped to tackle more advanced projects and to continue your exploration of scalable, efficient programming. Your journey with Go is just beginning, and with each project and challenge, you will grow more confident in your abilities.

Chapter 3: Diving into Go Fundamentals

1. Introduction

In modern programming, mastering the fundamentals is the key to building robust, scalable, and maintainable software. In this chapter, we delve into the core elements of the Go programming language. Whether you are just beginning your coding journey, a professional developer seeking to broaden your toolkit, or a hobbyist experimenting with new ideas, understanding these fundamentals will empower you to build complex applications with ease.

At the heart of Go lies a philosophy of simplicity and efficiency. Its built-in support for concurrency, minimalistic syntax, and strong performance make it a popular choice for a wide range of applications—from microservices and web servers to command-line utilities and data processing tools. In this chapter, we will explore three critical areas:

1. **Data Structures:**
    Learn about arrays, slices, maps, and structs—the fundamental building blocks for storing and organizing data. We will examine how these structures work, their use cases, and how they interrelate.

2. **Control Flow & Functions:**
    Discover how to direct the execution of your programs with if statements, loops, and switch-case constructs. We also cover function basics, explaining how to modularize your code, improve reusability, and enhance readability.

3. **Pointers and Memory Management:**
    Dive into the intricacies of pointers and references. Understand how Go handles memory automatically with its garbage collection while still offering powerful tools for fine-tuning performance through pointer manipulation.

Why Should You Care?

Understanding these fundamentals is not just about learning syntax; it's about developing the mental models that underpin effective software design. Imagine having a toolbox where each tool is perfectly suited for a specific job. By mastering Go's data structures and control mechanisms, you equip yourself with the tools necessary to solve real-world problems in a clean, efficient, and maintainable way.

Key Terminology

Before we begin, let's define some essential terms:

- **Array:** A fixed-length sequence of elements of a specific type.

- **Slice:** A dynamically-sized, flexible view into the elements of an array.

- **Map:** A collection of key-value pairs for fast lookup.

- **Struct:** A composite data type that groups together variables under one name.

- **Control Flow:** The order in which individual statements, instructions, or function calls are executed.

- **Pointer:** A variable that holds the memory address of another variable.

- **Garbage Collection:** An automatic memory management feature that frees memory occupied by objects that are no longer in use.

Setting the Tone

Throughout this chapter, our goal is to provide clarity and practical insights. We will use real-world analogies and step-by-step examples to break down complex ideas into understandable concepts. Whether you prefer visual aids like diagrams and flowcharts or code examples that you can run and experiment with, this chapter aims to offer a comprehensive, engaging, and professional guide to Go's core fundamentals.

2. Core Concepts and Theory

In this section, we break down the core concepts that form the backbone of Go programming. We start with data structures—arrays, slices, maps, and structs—then move to control flow constructs and functions, and finally examine pointers and memory management.

2.1 Data Structures

Arrays

Arrays in Go are fixed-size sequences that hold elements of a single type. They provide predictable memory allocation and are ideal when the number of elements is known ahead of time.

Example:

```go
package main

import "fmt"

func main() {
    // Declare an array of five integers
    var numbers [5]int = [5]int{10, 20, 30, 40, 50}
    fmt.Println("Array:", numbers)
}
```

Explanation:
Here, we declare an array named numbers that can hold five integers. Arrays are useful when you have a fixed collection of items.

Analogy:
Think of an array as a row of mailboxes, each with a fixed position. You know exactly where each mailbox is, and the number of mailboxes never changes.

Slices

Slices are a more flexible abstraction built on top of arrays. They allow dynamic resizing and are the most commonly used data structure in Go.

Example:

```go
package main

import "fmt"

func main() {
    // Create a slice of integers
    numbers := []int{10, 20, 30, 40, 50}
    fmt.Println("Slice:", numbers)

    // Append a new element
    numbers = append(numbers, 60)
    fmt.Println("After appending:", numbers)
}
```

Explanation:
Unlike arrays, slices can grow or shrink dynamically. The append function is used to add elements to a slice. Internally, slices maintain a pointer to an underlying array.

Visual Aid Suggestion:
A diagram showing an array with fixed size and a slice that overlays part of that array and then expands into a new, larger array when necessary.

Maps

Maps in Go are key-value stores, providing an efficient way to look up values based on keys. They are similar to dictionaries in other programming languages.

Example:

```go
package main

import "fmt"

func main() {
    // Declare and initialize a map
    ages := map[string]int{
        "Alice": 30,
```

```go
        "Bob":     25,
        "Carol": 27,
    }
    fmt.Println("Map of ages:", ages)

    // Access a value
    fmt.Println("Alice's age:", ages["Alice"])

    // Add a new key-value pair
    ages["Dave"] = 35
    fmt.Println("Updated Map:", ages)
}
```

Explanation:
Maps are ideal for scenarios where you need fast lookups. In this example, names are used as keys to store and retrieve ages.

Real-World Application:
Consider a scenario where you manage user data in an application. Maps can be used to store user profiles keyed by unique identifiers, allowing quick access to user information.

Structs

Structs are custom data types that group together fields. They are similar to records or objects in other languages and are used to represent complex entities.

Example:

```go
go

package main

import "fmt"

// Person defines a structure for a person
type Person struct {
    Name string
    Age  int
}

func main() {
    // Create an instance of Person
    person := Person{Name: "Alice", Age: 30}
```

```
fmt.Println("Person:", person)
}
```

Explanation:
A struct allows you to combine different types of data into a single entity. Here, Person has two fields: Name and Age.

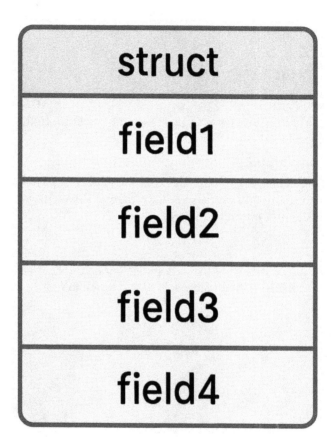

2.2 Control Flow & Functions

Conditional Statements

Control flow constructs are the building blocks of decision-making in programming.

If Statements:

```go
package main

import "fmt"

func main() {
    age := 20
    if age >= 18 {
        fmt.Println("You are an adult.")
    } else {
        fmt.Println("You are a minor.")
    }
}
```

Explanation:
This example uses an if-else statement to check a condition and execute different code based on the outcome.

Analogy:
Conditional statements are like decision points in a road map—they determine which path to take based on current conditions.

Loops

Loops enable repetitive execution of code blocks until a certain condition is met.

For Loop Example:

```go
package main

import "fmt"

func main() {
    for i := 1; i <= 5; i++ {
        fmt.Printf("Iteration %d\n", i)
    }
}
```

Explanation:
The for loop in Go is versatile and can be used as a traditional loop, a while loop, or even a range-based loop for iterating over collections.

Switch Statements

Switch statements simplify multi-branch decision-making by comparing a value against several cases.

Example:

```go
package main

import "fmt"

func main() {
    day := "Tuesday"
    switch day {
    case "Monday":
        fmt.Println("Start of the work week.")
    case "Friday":
        fmt.Println("End of the work week.")
    default:
        fmt.Println("Midweek days.")
    }
}
```

Explanation:
This switch statement evaluates the variable day and executes the corresponding case. If none match, it falls back to the default.

Functions

Functions encapsulate logic into reusable blocks. They improve modularity, readability, and maintainability of your code.

Basic Function Example:

```go
package main

import "fmt"
```

```go
// add returns the sum of two integers.
func add(a, b int) int {
    return a + b
}

func main() {
    result := add(10, 15)
    fmt.Printf("The sum is: %d\n", result)
}
```

Explanation:
This function takes two integers as input and returns their sum. Functions can be called multiple times, making them ideal for repetitive tasks.

Analogy:
A function is like a recipe that you can follow over and over. Once you know the steps, you can reuse them to prepare the same dish without rethinking the entire process.

2.3 Pointers and Memory Management

Understanding Pointers

Pointers are variables that store the memory address of another variable. They allow you to directly manipulate memory and can improve performance by avoiding unnecessary ing of data.

Pointer Example:

```go
go

package main

import "fmt"

func main() {
    // Declare an integer variable
    num := 42

    // Create a pointer to num
    ptr := &num

    fmt.Println("Value of num:", num)
    fmt.Println("Memory address of num:", ptr)
    fmt.Println("Dereferenced value:", *ptr)
```

}

Explanation:
In this example, the operator & obtains the memory address of num, and * is used to dereference the pointer. Pointers are especially useful when you need to pass large data structures to functions without ing them.

Analogy:
Imagine a pointer as a signpost that directs you to a particular building (the variable). Instead of carrying the building with you, you simply refer to its address.

Memory Management and Garbage Collection

Go provides automatic memory management through garbage collection. This means that you don't need to manually allocate and free memory—the runtime takes care of it.

Example:

```go
package main

import "fmt"

func main() {
    // Allocate memory for a slice
    data := []int{1, 2, 3, 4, 5}
    fmt.Println("Data:", data)
}
```

Explanation:
When data goes out of scope, the garbage collector will automatically free the memory. This reduces the risk of memory leaks and simplifies development.

Advanced Pointer Concepts

Pointers can also be used in more advanced ways, such as modifying data in functions and working with structures.

Modifying Data via Pointers:

```go
```

```go
package main

import "fmt"

// increment increases the value by 1.
func increment(n *int) {
    *n = *n + 1
}

func main() {
    value := 10
    fmt.Println("Before increment:", value)
    increment(&value)
    fmt.Println("After increment:", value)
}
```

Explanation:
Here, the function increment takes a pointer to an integer, modifies the value at that address, and reflects the change outside the function scope.

---

3. Tools and Setup

Even though this chapter focuses on Go fundamentals, having a proper environment is crucial for effective learning and experimentation. In this section, we review the essential tools and best practices for setting up your Go development environment, with an emphasis on ensuring that you can run, test, and debug the code examples presented here.

Essential Tools

- **Go Compiler and Runtime:**
  Download the latest version from the official Go website. This package includes the compiler, runtime, and standard libraries.

- **IDE or Text Editor:**
  Recommended choices include Visual Studio Code, GoLand, or Sublime Text with Go plugins. These tools offer syntax highlighting, auto-completion, and integrated debugging.

- **Version Control:**
  Git is widely used. Install Git from git-scm.com to manage your code and collaborate with others.

- **Terminal:**
  Familiarize yourself with your operating system's command line for running Go commands and scripts.

Environment Setup: Step-by-Step

3.1 Installing Go

1. **Download and Install:**
   Navigate to the Go download page and select the installer for your operating system. Run the installer and follow the instructions.

2. **Verify Installation:**
   Open a terminal and run:

bash

```
go version
```

This should output the version of Go you installed.

```
~$ go versiion
go go1.21.arm64
```

3.2 Configuring Your Workspace

Go organizes code in a workspace that includes directories such as src, pkg, and bin. To create a workspace:

```bash
mkdir -p $HOME/go/{src,pkg,bin}
```
Set your GOPATH environment variable by adding the following to your shell configuration file:

```bash
export GOPATH=$HOME/go
export PATH=$PATH:$GOPATH/bin
```
Reload the configuration:

```bash
source ~/.bashrc
```

3.3 IDE Setup

Using an IDE like Visual Studio Code enhances productivity:

- **Install VS Code:**
  Download it from the official website.

- **Install Go Extension:**
  Open the Extensions panel in VS Code, search for "Go," and install the official extension.

- **Configure the Extension:**
  Follow any prompts to install additional tools such as gopls for language support.

```
main.go
1    package main
2    import "fmt"
3
4    func main() {
5        fmt.Println(Hello, Go")
6    }

     1 error: 1:3: fmt.Println not declared
     by package fmt

     ⊟ Println
     ⊘ Print
     ⊟ PrintValues
     {:} Bytes
     ⊙ Duration
```

Additional Tools
- **Debugging Tools:**
  The Go extension integrates debugging features. Learn to set breakpoints and inspect variables.

- **Documentation:**
  Tools like GoDoc generate documentation from your comments, promoting clean and maintainable code.

By ensuring your environment is properly set up, you're ready to dive into the hands-on projects in the next section. This setup not only facilitates smooth coding sessions but also reinforces best practices in managing a Go project.

4. Hands-on Examples & Projects

In this section, we translate theory into practice. We will build several projects that progressively incorporate the fundamentals of data structures, control flow, functions, and pointer manipulation. Each project includes detailed explanations, clean code, and ideas for visual aids.

Project 1: Data Structures Playground

4.1 Exploring Arrays, Slices, Maps, and Structs

Create a new file named dataplayground.go and enter the following code:

```go
package main

import "fmt"

// Define a struct for a Book
type Book struct {
    Title  string
    Author string
    Pages  int
}

func main() {
    // Arrays: fixed-size collection
    var numbers [5]int = [5]int{10, 20, 30, 40, 50}
    fmt.Println("Array:", numbers)

    // Slices: dynamic, flexible view into an array
    fruits := []string{"apple", "banana", "cherry"}
    fruits = append(fruits, "date")
    fmt.Println("Slice:", fruits)

    // Maps: key-value pairs for quick lookups
    capitals := map[string]string{
        "France":  "Paris",
        "Germany": "Berlin",
        "Japan":   "Tokyo",
    }
    capitals["Italy"] = "Rome"
```

```go
    fmt.Println("Map of Capitals:", capitals)

    // Structs: custom composite data types
    book := Book{Title: "Go in Action", Author:
"William Kennedy", Pages: 300}
    fmt.Printf("Book Details: %+v\n", book)
}
```

Explanation:

This project illustrates the creation and manipulation of arrays, slices, maps, and structs. You can extend it by adding more operations—like iterating over the map or modifying struct fields.

Project 2: Control Flow and Function Workshop

4.2 Building a Utility to Process Data

Create a file named controlfunctions.go:

```go
package main

import "fmt"

// max returns the maximum of two integers.
func max(a, b int) int {
    if a > b {
        return a
    }
    return b
}

// sum returns the sum of all elements in a slice.
func sum(numbers []int) int {
    total := 0
    for _, num := range numbers {
        total += num
    }
    return total
}

func main() {
    // Using if statements and function calls
```

```
    a, b := 45, 32
    fmt.Printf("Max of %d and %d is %d\n", a, b,
max(a, b))

    // For loop to sum slice elements
    nums := []int{5, 10, 15, 20, 25}
    fmt.Printf("Sum of %v is %d\n", nums, sum(nums))

    // Demonstrate switch-case: categorize the sum
    total := sum(nums)
    switch {
    case total < 50:
        fmt.Println("Low total")
    case total < 100:
        fmt.Println("Medium total")
    default:
        fmt.Println("High total")
    }
}
```

Explanation:

This utility demonstrates how functions encapsulate logic and how control flow structures—if statements, loops, and switch—manage decision-making. Running this code will show the max value, the sum of numbers, and a category for the sum.

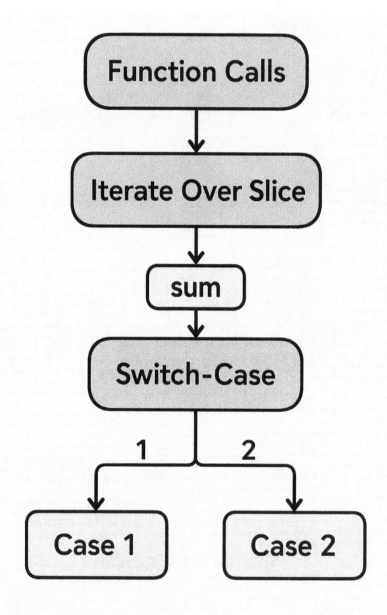

Project 3: Exploring Pointers and Memory Management

4.3 Pointer Manipulation and Safe Memory Practices

Create a file named pointers.go:

```go
package main

import "fmt"

// updateValue demonstrates modifying a value using a
pointer.
func updateValue(val *int) {
    *val = *val + 100
}

func main() {
    // Declare a variable and a pointer to it
    number := 50
    fmt.Printf("Initial value: %d\n", number)

    // Pass the pointer to the function
    updateValue(&number)
    fmt.Printf("After update: %d\n", number)

    // Demonstrate pointer with structs
    type Person struct {
        Name string
        Age  int
    }
    alice := Person{Name: "Alice", Age: 28}
    // Create a pointer to the struct
    pAlice := &alice
    pAlice.Age = 29
    fmt.Printf("Updated Person: %+v\n", alice)
}
```

Explanation:

This example shows how pointers let you modify data directly. Notice how the updateValue function takes a pointer to an integer, updates its value, and those changes persist outside the function. We also demonstrate pointer usage with structs.

Project 4: Integrating Concepts into a Mini Application

4.4 Building a Simple Inventory Management System

Create a file named inventory.go:

```go
package main

import (
    "fmt"
)

// Product defines a struct for an item in inventory.
type Product struct {
    ID       int
    Name     string
    Quantity int
}

// updateStock uses a pointer to modify product quantity.
func updateStock(p *Product, amount int) {
    p.Quantity += amount
}

func main() {
    // Initialize a slice of products
    inventory := []Product{
        {ID: 101, Name: "Laptop", Quantity: 10},
        {ID: 102, Name: "Smartphone", Quantity: 25},
        {ID: 103, Name: "Tablet", Quantity: 15},
    }

    // Display initial inventory
    fmt.Println("Initial Inventory:")
    for _, product := range inventory {
        fmt.Printf("ID: %d, Name: %s, Quantity: %d\n", product.ID, product.Name, product.Quantity)
```

```
    }

    // Update stock for a product using pointer
    updateStock(&inventory[1], 5) // Add 5
smartphones

    // Display updated inventory
    fmt.Println("\nUpdated Inventory:")
    for _, product := range inventory {
        fmt.Printf("ID: %d, Name: %s, Quantity:
%d\n", product.ID, product.Name, product.Quantity)
    }
}
```

Explanation:
This mini application integrates data structures (slices and structs), control flow (loops for display), functions, and pointer usage to manage an inventory system. It demonstrates a real-world use case where inventory items are updated dynamically.

---

5. Advanced Techniques & Optimization

As you become more comfortable with Go fundamentals, you can explore advanced techniques to write more efficient and maintainable code. In this section, we cover best practices for code organization, advanced pointer techniques, and memory management optimizations.

5.1 Modular Code and Package Organization

Breaking your code into packages is essential for larger projects. Organizing functions, structs, and related operations into logical packages improves reusability and testability.

Example:
Imagine refactoring the inventory system by creating a dedicated package named inventory with its own set of functions. This modular approach can simplify maintenance as your project grows.

5.2 Advanced Pointer Usage

Beyond basic pointer manipulation, advanced techniques involve pointer arithmetic, careful use of nil pointers, and avoiding common pitfalls such as dangling pointers.

Best Practice:
Always check if a pointer is nil before dereferencing it, to prevent runtime panics.

go

```go
if p != nil {
    fmt.Println("Pointer is valid:", *p)
} else {
    fmt.Println("Pointer is nil.")
}
```

5.3 Memory Optimization

Go's garbage collector handles memory management automatically, but you can optimize performance by reducing unnecessary allocations. Use slices efficiently by preallocating capacity, and avoid creating temporary objects inside loops.

Example:
Preallocate a slice to avoid multiple memory reallocations:

go

```go
func processData(data []int) []int {
    results := make([]int, 0, len(data))
    for _, v := range data {
        results = append(results, v*2)
    }
    return results
}
```

5.4 Performance Profiling

Use Go's built-in profiling tools (such as pprof) to identify bottlenecks in your code. Profiling helps determine which functions are most resource-intensive and guides your optimization efforts.

Tip:
Add a simple profiler in your code to generate performance reports that help you decide where to optimize.

---

6. Troubleshooting and Problem-Solving

Every programmer encounters bugs and challenges. In this section, we discuss common issues related to Go fundamentals and provide troubleshooting strategies.

6.1 Common Pitfalls

- **Index Out of Range:**
  When working with arrays or slices, ensure that you do not access an index that does not exist. Use the built-in len function to verify boundaries.

- **Nil Pointer Dereference:**
  Always check if pointers are nil before using them.

- **Type Mismatch:**
  Go's static typing can lead to compilation errors if data types do not match. Read error messages carefully to fix type-related issues.

6.2 Debugging Strategies

- **Verbose Logging:**
  Use fmt.Printf or the log package to print variable values at critical points in your code.

- **Use the Go Race Detector:**
  For concurrent code, run your program with the -race flag to catch race conditions:

```bash
go run -race yourprogram.go
```

- **Incremental Testing:**
  Test functions individually before integrating them into larger applications.

Before-and-After Example:

Imagine a function that crashes due to a nil pointer. Adding a simple nil check improves reliability:

```go
if ptr == nil {
    fmt.Println("Error: nil pointer encountered.")
    return
}
```

6.3 Collaborative Problem-Solving

Peer reviews and code walkthroughs are valuable. Explaining your code to another developer can reveal issues that you might have overlooked.

```python
→  ☰  main.py

4      def calculate_sum(a, b):
5          total = a + b
7    ● x = x = 10        ↖5
8      return x = 5
9      result calculate_sum(x, y)
10
```

Frames

```
1  ▼  calculate_sum  main.py:7
```

Variables

```
a  =  10
b  =  5
total  =  15
x  =  10
```

7. Conclusion & Next Steps

In this chapter, we explored the fundamental building blocks of Go that form the foundation of all advanced programming in the language. From data structures like arrays, slices, maps, and structs, to control flow constructs and functions, and finally to the intricacies of pointers and

memory management, you now have a comprehensive understanding of
Go's core mechanics.

Key Takeaways

- **Data Structures:**
  Arrays provide fixed storage, slices offer dynamic flexibility, maps
  enable fast lookups, and structs let you model complex data. Each
  of these tools plays a crucial role in organizing data effectively.

- **Control Flow & Functions:**
  Mastering if statements, loops, and switch cases allows you to
  control program execution, while functions let you encapsulate
  logic and improve code modularity.

- **Pointers and Memory Management:**
  Pointers enable efficient memory manipulation and function
  parameter passing, while Go's garbage collection ensures that
  memory management remains largely transparent and safe.

Reflecting on Your Learning

By combining theory with practical projects—from a data structures
playground to a mini inventory management system—you have applied
these core concepts in real-world scenarios. This hands-on approach not
only solidifies your understanding but also prepares you to tackle more
advanced topics in Go.

Next Steps

As you continue your journey with Go, consider exploring:

- **Concurrency and Parallelism:**
  Learn about goroutines and channels to write high-performance,
  concurrent programs.

- **Advanced Go Patterns:**
  Investigate design patterns, modularization, and package
  management to build larger and more maintainable projects.

- **Real-World Applications:**
  Apply your skills in areas such as web development,
  microservices, and data processing.

Final Thoughts

Understanding these fundamentals is a critical milestone on your journey as a Go developer. The concepts discussed in this chapter serve as the building blocks for more complex systems. With practice and continuous learning, you will be well-equipped to design, build, and optimize efficient, scalable applications in Go.

As you move forward, revisit these core concepts often. Experiment with the provided code examples, extend them, and try integrating new features. Every challenge you encounter is an opportunity to deepen your understanding and refine your skills.

Chapter 4: Concurrency in Go

This chapter is dedicated to one of Go's most celebrated features: concurrency. In today's computing landscape—where scalability and efficient resource utilization are paramount—understanding concurrency is essential. Go has been designed with concurrency as a first-class citizen, and its lightweight threads, known as goroutines, along with powerful communication primitives called channels, allow developers to build high-performance, concurrent applications with relative ease. In this chapter, we cover the following major topics:

- **Goroutines:** Introduction to lightweight threads, why they are important, and how they enhance scalability.

- **Channels:** The mechanism for safe communication between goroutines, accompanied by practical examples.

- **Concurrency Patterns:** Exploration of worker pools, fan-out/fan-in architectures, and real-world use cases to solidify your understanding.

This comprehensive guide is intended for beginners, seasoned professionals, and hobbyists alike. Whether you're stepping into concurrency for the first time or looking to optimize and fine-tune your concurrent Go applications, this chapter offers a deep dive into theory, practical setups, and hands-on projects.

1. Introduction

Modern software applications must often perform multiple tasks simultaneously—whether it's handling numerous client requests on a web server, processing data streams in real time, or simply managing background tasks while keeping the user interface responsive. Traditional threading models can be complex, error-prone, and resource-intensive. Go addresses these challenges head-on with its innovative approach to concurrency.

Why Concurrency Matters

Concurrency is the art of managing multiple tasks at the same time. In the context of Go, this is achieved through **goroutines**—functions that can run concurrently with other functions. Unlike heavyweight threads found in many other languages, goroutines are extremely lightweight. This means you can spawn thousands (or even millions) of them without overwhelming your system's resources. The simplicity and efficiency of goroutines make Go an attractive choice for building scalable, high-performance applications.

Key Concepts and Terminology

Before diving deeper, let's clarify some key concepts:

- **Goroutine:** A lightweight thread managed by the Go runtime. Initiated with the go keyword, goroutines enable concurrent execution of functions.

- **Channel:** A conduit through which goroutines can communicate safely. Channels help avoid race conditions by ensuring that data exchanges occur in a synchronized manner.

- **Concurrency Patterns:** Reusable solutions for common problems in concurrent programming. Examples include worker pools and fan-out/fan-in patterns.

- **Scalability:** The capability of a system to handle increasing loads by distributing tasks efficiently across available resources.

Setting the Tone

Throughout this chapter, you will encounter practical examples that illustrate the power of Go's concurrency model. We start with an introduction to goroutines, move into channel-based communication, and then explore real-world concurrency patterns. Each section builds on the previous one, ensuring that by the end, you have a clear understanding of not only how concurrency works in Go but also how to apply these techniques in your projects.

Imagine a bustling kitchen where multiple chefs work in parallel to prepare a meal. Each chef (goroutine) is responsible for a specific task, and they coordinate via clear communication channels (channels) to ensure that the meal is served on time. This is the essence of Go's approach to concurrency—efficient, coordinated, and scalable.

---

2. Core Concepts and Theory

In this section, we dissect the fundamental building blocks of concurrency in Go. We start by exploring goroutines, then move to channels, and finally discuss common concurrency patterns that are essential for building scalable applications.

2.1 Goroutines: Lightweight Threads

Goroutines are the cornerstone of Go's concurrency model. They are functions that run concurrently with other functions. Initiating a goroutine is as simple as prefixing a function call with the go keyword. The Go runtime manages the scheduling and execution of these goroutines, enabling you to write concurrent code without having to manage system threads manually.

Example: Basic Goroutine

```go
go

package main

import (
    "fmt"
    "time"
)

func greet(name string) {
    fmt.Printf("Hello, %s!\n", name)
}

func main() {
    // Start a new goroutine
    go greet("Alice")

    // Give the goroutine time to execute before main
exits.
    time.Sleep(100 * time.Millisecond)
}
```

Explanation:
In the example above, the greet function is executed as a goroutine. Note that the time.Sleep call in main is used to allow the goroutine to finish executing before the program terminates. In real-world applications, proper synchronization (using channels or wait groups) would be used instead of sleep.

Analogy:
Think of goroutines as the many virtual assistants you can hire to perform small tasks concurrently. They're inexpensive in terms of resources and can be deployed in large numbers to handle multiple tasks simultaneously.

2.2 Channels: Communication Between Goroutines

While goroutines allow functions to run concurrently, channels provide the mechanism for these goroutines to communicate. A channel in Go is a typed conduit through which you can send and receive values. Channels help prevent common concurrency issues like race conditions by ensuring that only one goroutine can access the shared data at a time.

Example: Using Channels

```go
package main

import "fmt"

func sum(numbers []int, result chan int) {
    total := 0
    for _, num := range numbers {
        total += num
    }
    // Send the computed sum to the channel.
    result <- total
}

func main() {
    nums := []int{1, 2, 3, 4, 5}
    resultChan := make(chan int)

    // Start a goroutine to calculate the sum.
```

```go
go sum(nums, resultChan)

// Receive the result from the channel.
sumResult := <-resultChan
fmt.Println("Sum:", sumResult)
}
```

Explanation:

The sum function calculates the total of a slice of integers and sends the result back via a channel. In main, we create a channel, start the goroutine, and then wait to receive the result. This pattern ensures that data is passed safely between concurrently running functions.

2.3 Concurrency Patterns

Once you understand goroutines and channels, you can apply several common concurrency patterns to solve real-world problems more elegantly.

Worker Pools

A worker pool is a pattern where a fixed number of goroutines (workers) process jobs from a queue. This pattern is useful when you have a large number of tasks that need to be processed concurrently but want to limit the number of concurrent operations to control resource usage.

Example: Worker Pool

```go
go

package main

import (
    "fmt"
    "sync"
    "time"
)

// job represents a unit of work.
type job struct {
    id int
}

// worker processes jobs from the job channel.
```

```go
func worker(id int, jobs <-chan job, wg
*sync.WaitGroup) {
    defer wg.Done()
    for j := range jobs {
        fmt.Printf("Worker %d processing job %d\n",
id, j.id)
        time.Sleep(100 * time.Millisecond) //
Simulate work
    }
}

func main() {
    const numWorkers = 3
    const numJobs = 10

    jobs := make(chan job, numJobs)
    var wg sync.WaitGroup

    // Start worker goroutines.
    for i := 1; i <= numWorkers; i++ {
        wg.Add(1)
        go worker(i, jobs, &wg)
    }

    // Send jobs to the workers.
    for j := 1; j <= numJobs; j++ {
        jobs <- job{id: j}
    }
    close(jobs)

    // Wait for all workers to finish.
    wg.Wait()
    fmt.Println("All jobs processed.")
}
```

Explanation:

This worker pool example creates a channel to distribute jobs to a fixed number of worker goroutines. The sync.WaitGroup is used to ensure that main waits for all workers to complete their tasks.

Real-World Application:

Worker pools are widely used in server applications where requests must be handled concurrently without overwhelming the system. For example, a web server might use a worker pool to process HTTP requests efficiently.

Fan-Out / Fan-In

The fan-out/fan-in pattern is a concurrency model where work is distributed (fanned out) to multiple goroutines, and the results are gathered (fanned in) to a single channel. This pattern is useful when you need to process parts of a task in parallel and then combine the results.

Example: Fan-Out / Fan-In

```go
package main

import (
    "fmt"
    "sync"
    "time"
)

func process(data int, results chan<- int, wg
*sync.WaitGroup) {
    defer wg.Done()
    // Simulate processing time.
    time.Sleep(50 * time.Millisecond)
    results <- data * data // Return square of the
number.
}

func main() {
    input := []int{2, 4, 6, 8, 10}
    results := make(chan int, len(input))
    var wg sync.WaitGroup

    // Fan-out: Start a goroutine for each piece of
data.
    for _, num := range input {
        wg.Add(1)
        go process(num, results, &wg)
    }

    // Fan-in: Close the results channel after all
processing is done.
    go func() {
        wg.Wait()
```

```
        close(results)
    }()

    // Read and print results.
    for res := range results {
        fmt.Println("Result:", res)
    }
}
```

Explanation:
Each number in the input slice is processed concurrently to compute its square. The results are sent to a common channel, which is then read sequentially in main.

Real-World Concurrency Use Cases

Concurrency isn't just an academic exercise—it's a critical component in many real-world systems:

- **Web Servers:**
  Handling multiple client connections concurrently.

- **Data Processing Pipelines:**
  Processing large volumes of data in parallel to reduce latency.

- **Real-Time Analytics:**
  Concurrently collecting and processing streaming data for immediate insights.

- **Distributed Systems:**
  Coordinating tasks across multiple nodes efficiently.

3. Tools and Setup

Before experimenting with concurrency, ensure that your development environment is properly set up to support efficient Go development. In this section, we list the tools you'll need and provide detailed instructions for configuring your system.

Essential Tools for Concurrency

- **Go Compiler and Runtime:**
  Download the latest version of Go from the official website. This

installation includes the compiler, runtime, and all necessary standard libraries.

- **IDE or Text Editor:**
  Use an IDE such as Visual Studio Code or GoLand, which offer excellent support for debugging and code completion.

- **Version Control (Git):**
  Git is essential for managing your project's source code and collaborating with others.

- **Terminal/Command Line Interface:**
  A reliable terminal is crucial for running Go commands, managing build processes, and debugging.

Environment Setup: Step-by-Step

3.1 Installing Go

1. **Download and Install:**
   Go to the Go downloads page, select the installer for your operating system, and run it.

2. **Verify Installation:**
   Open your terminal and run:

```bash

```

```bash
go version
```
Confirm that the output displays the correct version.

3.2 Configuring Your Workspace

Go projects typically use a workspace that contains directories such as src, pkg, and bin. Create your workspace as follows:

```bash

```

```bash
mkdir -p $HOME/go/{src,pkg,bin}
```
Then, set the GOPATH environment variable by adding these lines to your shell configuration file (e.g., .bashrc or .zshrc):

```bash

```

```bash
export GOPATH=$HOME/go
```

```
export PATH=$PATH:$GOPATH/bin
```
Reload your shell configuration:

```
bash
```

```
source ~/.bashrc
```

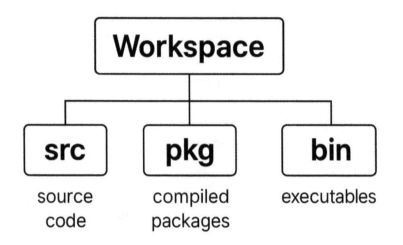

3.3 IDE Setup for Concurrency

A good IDE enhances productivity by providing features such as syntax highlighting, code navigation, and integrated debugging.

- **Visual Studio Code:**

    1. Download and install VS Code.

    2. Open VS Code and navigate to the Extensions pane.

    3. Search for the "Go" extension and install it.

    4. Follow any additional prompts (e.g., installing gopls for language support).

Additional Tools for Debugging

- **Race Detector:**
  Use Go's built-in race detector with the -race flag to identify data races.

- **pprof:**
  Profiling tools such as pprof help diagnose performance bottlenecks in concurrent programs.

---

4. Hands-on Examples & Projects

Theory comes to life through practical examples. In this section, you will build projects that utilize goroutines, channels, and concurrency patterns to solve real-world problems.

Project 1: Basic Goroutine Demonstration

4.1 Launching Multiple Goroutines

Create a file named goroutines_demo.go:

```go
package main

import (
    "fmt"
    "time"
)

func printMessage(id int) {
    fmt.Printf("Goroutine %d: Hello from concurrent
execution!\n", id)
}

func main() {
    for i := 1; i <= 5; i++ {
        go printMessage(i)
    }
    // Wait for goroutines to complete.
    time.Sleep(200 * time.Millisecond)
}
```

Explanation:
This example launches five goroutines concurrently. Each goroutine prints a message along with its identifier. Although we use a simple sleep to allow completion, real-world applications should use synchronization primitives like wait groups.

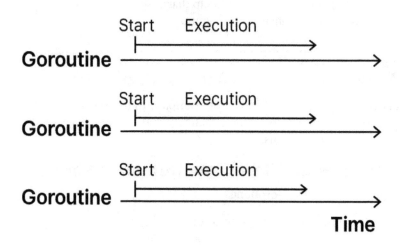

Project 2: Channel-Based Communication
4.2 Synchronized Data Exchange

Create a file named channels_demo.go:

```go
package main

import "fmt"

func square(n int, ch chan int) {
    ch <- n * n
}

func main() {
    ch := make(chan int)
    go square(5, ch)
```

```go
    result := <-ch
    fmt.Printf("Square of 5 is %d\n", result)
}
```

Explanation:
The square function calculates the square of a number and sends the result through a channel. The main function receives the result from the channel, ensuring safe communication between the goroutine and the main thread.

Project 3: Implementing a Worker Pool
4.3 Worker Pool for Job Processing

Create a file named worker_pool.go:

```go
package main

import (
    "fmt"
    "sync"
    "time"
)

// Job represents a unit of work.
type Job struct {
    ID int
}

// worker processes jobs received from the jobs
channel.
func worker(id int, jobs <-chan Job, wg
*sync.WaitGroup) {
    defer wg.Done()
    for job := range jobs {
        fmt.Printf("Worker %d processing job %d\n",
id, job.ID)
        time.Sleep(100 * time.Millisecond) //
Simulate work.
    }
}

func main() {
```

```go
const numWorkers = 3
const numJobs = 10

jobs := make(chan Job, numJobs)
var wg sync.WaitGroup

// Launch workers.
for i := 1; i <= numWorkers; i++ {
    wg.Add(1)
    go worker(i, jobs, &wg)
}

// Send jobs to the worker pool.
for j := 1; j <= numJobs; j++ {
    jobs <- Job{ID: j}
}
close(jobs)

// Wait for all workers to finish.
wg.Wait()
fmt.Println("All jobs processed.")
}
```

Explanation:

This project implements a worker pool where multiple worker goroutines process jobs from a shared channel. The use of a wait group ensures that the main function waits for all jobs to be processed before terminating.

Project 4: Fan-Out / Fan-In Pattern

4.4 Parallel Processing with Result Aggregation

Create a file named fan_in_fan_out.go:

```go
go

package main

import (
    "fmt"
    "sync"
    "time"
)
```

```
func processData(n int, results chan<- int, wg
*sync.WaitGroup) {
    defer wg.Done()
    time.Sleep(50 * time.Millisecond)
    results <- n * n
}

func main() {
    data := []int{2, 4, 6, 8, 10}
    results := make(chan int, len(data))
    var wg sync.WaitGroup

    // Fan-out: Start a goroutine for each data
element.
    for _, n := range data {
        wg.Add(1)
        go processData(n, results, &wg)
    }

    // Fan-in: Close the results channel after
processing.
    go func() {
        wg.Wait()
        close(results)
    }()

    // Collect and print results.
    for res := range results {
        fmt.Println("Processed result:", res)
    }
}
```
Explanation:
This example demonstrates the fan-out/fan-in pattern. Data elements are processed concurrently, and the results are gathered through a common channel.

5. Advanced Techniques & Optimization

Once you are comfortable with the basics of concurrency in Go, you can explore advanced techniques that further optimize performance and improve code maintainability.

5.1 Optimizing Goroutine Usage

- **Avoiding Leaks:**
  Ensure that goroutines exit properly by using channels or context cancellation.

- **Using Wait Groups:**
  The sync.WaitGroup is indispensable for coordinating goroutines without resorting to arbitrary sleep durations.

Example: Using Context for Cancellation

```go
go

package main

import (
    "context"
    "fmt"
    "time"
)

func doWork(ctx context.Context, id int) {
    for {
        select {
        case <-ctx.Done():
            fmt.Printf("Worker %d: stopping work\n",
id)
            return
        default:
            fmt.Printf("Worker %d: working...\n", id)
            time.Sleep(100 * time.Millisecond)
        }
    }
}

func main() {
    ctx, cancel :=
context.WithTimeout(context.Background(),
500*time.Millisecond)
    defer cancel()

    for i := 1; i <= 3; i++ {
        go doWork(ctx, i)
```

```
    }

    time.Sleep(1 * time.Second)
    fmt.Println("Main function done.")
}
```

Explanation:
This example demonstrates how to use context cancellation to gracefully stop goroutines. This prevents resource leaks in long-running applications.

5.2 Advanced Channel Patterns

- **Buffered Channels:**
  Use buffered channels to allow a limited number of values to be sent without an immediate receiver.

- **Channel Directionality:**
  Restrict channels to sending or receiving to enforce better code contracts.

- **Pipeline Processing:**
  Build processing pipelines where each stage is handled by a different goroutine.

Example: Pipeline Processing

```go
package main

import "fmt"

func stage1(input []int, out chan<- int) {
    for _, v := range input {
        out <- v + 1
    }
    close(out)
}

func stage2(in <-chan int, out chan<- int) {
    for v := range in {
        out <- v * 2
    }
    close(out)
}
```

```
func main() {
    input := []int{1, 2, 3, 4, 5}
    stage1Out := make(chan int, len(input))
    stage2Out := make(chan int, len(input))

    go stage1(input, stage1Out)
    go stage2(stage1Out, stage2Out)

    for result := range stage2Out {
        fmt.Println("Pipeline result:", result)
    }
}
```

Explanation:
Here, two stages of processing are linked via channels. This pattern is powerful when processing data streams in a series of steps.

5.3 Performance Profiling and Tuning

- **pprof:**
  Use Go's pprof package to profile CPU and memory usage.

- **Benchmarking:**
  Write benchmarks using Go's testing framework to measure the performance impact of your concurrency design.

Tip:
Always profile before and after optimizations to ensure that changes lead to improvements.

5.4 Best Practices for Concurrency

- **Keep Goroutines Small:**
  Write goroutines that do one thing and complete quickly.

- **Error Handling:**
  Ensure that errors in goroutines are handled properly, either by returning error values through channels or logging them.

- **Avoid Shared State:**
  Use channels to pass data instead of sharing memory between goroutines. This greatly reduces the likelihood of race conditions.

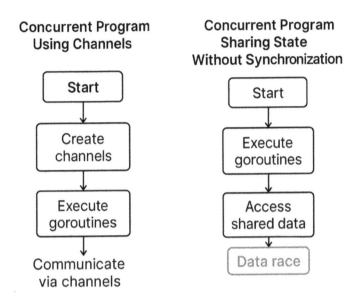

6. Troubleshooting and Problem-Solving

Even with a solid understanding of concurrency, challenges are inevitable. This section provides strategies and tips to troubleshoot common concurrency issues in Go.

6.1 Common Concurrency Pitfalls

- **Race Conditions:**
  When multiple goroutines access shared variables without proper synchronization.
  Solution: Use channels or the sync package (mutexes, wait groups) and run your code with the -race flag.

- **Deadlocks:**
  Occur when goroutines wait indefinitely for each other.
  Solution: Ensure that channels are properly closed and that every send has a corresponding receive.

- **Goroutine Leaks:**
  Occur when goroutines fail to exit, causing resource exhaustion.
  Solution: Use contexts, timeouts, or explicit cancellation signals.

6.2 Debugging Techniques

- **Verbose Logging:**
  Print statements or use the log package to trace the flow of execution.

- **Race Detector:**
  Run your programs with go run -race to catch data races early.

- **Incremental Testing:**
  Develop and test small, isolated components before integrating them into larger concurrent systems.

Before-and-After Example:
Imagine a scenario where a goroutine hangs because a channel is never closed. Adding proper closure and using a wait group fixes the issue.

6.3 Collaborative Debugging

Sometimes fresh eyes on your code can reveal issues that you might have missed. Code reviews and pair programming sessions can be highly effective when dealing with complex concurrent logic.

---

7. Conclusion & Next Steps

In this chapter, we have explored the power and elegance of concurrency in Go. We started by understanding the lightweight nature of goroutines, then delved into channels as the means for synchronized communication, and finally examined advanced concurrency patterns such as worker pools and fan-out/fan-in. Together, these features empower you to build scalable, efficient, and robust applications.

Key Takeaways

- **Goroutines:**
  Go's goroutines allow you to perform many tasks concurrently with minimal overhead. They are the building blocks of concurrent applications.

- **Channels:**
  Channels facilitate safe and structured communication between goroutines, reducing the risk of race conditions and ensuring synchronization.

- **Concurrency Patterns:**
  Patterns such as worker pools and fan-out/fan-in are essential tools for managing parallel workloads and aggregating results from multiple sources.

- **Optimization and Debugging:**
  Advanced techniques, including context cancellation, buffered channels, and profiling with pprof, enable you to fine-tune your concurrent programs and troubleshoot issues effectively.

Reflecting on Your Journey

By mastering these concurrency concepts, you've gained a significant advantage in designing high-performance applications. Whether you are developing a web server that handles thousands of simultaneous connections, processing large data sets in parallel, or creating responsive command-line tools, the principles discussed in this chapter are applicable to a wide range of real-world scenarios.

Next Steps

As you continue your exploration of Go, consider the following:

- **Dive Deeper into Concurrency Patterns:**
  Explore additional patterns such as the producer-consumer model, pipelines, and fan-out/fan-in with error handling.

- **Build Larger Projects:**
  Apply these concepts in building more complex systems. For instance, develop a concurrent web scraper, a real-time data processor, or a distributed task scheduler.

- **Engage with the Community:**
  The Go community is active and supportive. Participate in forums, contribute to open source projects, and share your experiences with others.

Final Thoughts

Concurrency in Go is more than just a language feature—it is a paradigm that enables developers to write efficient, scalable, and maintainable software. As you continue to experiment with goroutines and channels, remember that the key to mastering concurrency lies in understanding the flow of data and control between concurrent processes. Every bug you encounter is an opportunity to learn and improve your code.

With a solid grasp of these concepts, you are well-prepared to design and implement concurrent systems that can handle modern workloads gracefully. Embrace the power of concurrency and let it drive your next innovative project.

Chapter 5: Error Handling and Testing in Go

1. Introduction

In the ever-evolving world of software development, writing code that works is only half the battle. Ensuring that your code gracefully handles unexpected conditions and behaves as intended through rigorous testing is equally important. In Go, error handling and testing are treated as first-class citizens. Instead of relying on exceptions or complex error-handling frameworks, Go embraces simple, explicit, and idiomatic practices to manage errors and ensure code quality.

The Importance of Error Handling

Errors are an inevitable part of any application—from file I/O failures and network issues to user input mistakes. Proper error handling means detecting problems early, providing meaningful feedback, and preventing your application from crashing unexpectedly. In Go, errors are values that are returned from functions, allowing you to handle them in a straightforward and predictable manner. This approach encourages developers to think about error cases and write more resilient code.

Testing as a Pillar of Software Quality

Testing is the process of verifying that your code works as intended. It provides confidence when refactoring, adds documentation on how functions should behave, and serves as a safety net that catches regressions. Go's built-in testing package makes it easy to write unit tests, integration tests, and benchmarks. By integrating testing into your development workflow, you ensure that your applications remain robust and maintainable over time.

Key Concepts and Terminology

Before we dive deeper, let's clarify some key terms:

- **Error Handling:** The process of detecting and responding to errors in your code. In Go, this is typically done by returning an error value from a function.

- **Idiomatic Error Handling:** A set of conventions and best practices in Go that promotes clear and concise error management.

- **Custom Error Types:** User-defined types that implement the error interface, allowing you to add context to error messages.

- **Unit Testing:** Testing individual components or functions in isolation.

- **Integration Testing:** Testing how different components of an application work together.

- **Benchmarking:** Measuring the performance of code, often used to identify bottlenecks.

- **Test Coverage:** A measure of how much of your code is executed during testing.

Setting the Tone

Throughout this chapter, we will walk through error-handling strategies, explore how to write tests using Go's testing package, and provide hands-on examples that illustrate these concepts in action. Imagine your code as a finely tuned machine: robust error handling ensures that it continues running smoothly even when parts of it fail, while thorough testing acts as routine maintenance to keep the machine in top condition.

By the end of this chapter, you will have a comprehensive understanding of how to manage errors gracefully and verify your code through testing—key skills that will help you build high-quality, reliable Go applications.

2. Core Concepts and Theory

This section covers the foundational principles behind error handling and testing in Go. We'll explore idiomatic practices, custom error types, and various testing methodologies that ensure your code is robust and reliable.

2.1 Effective Error Handling

2.1.1 The Go Way of Handling Errors

Unlike some languages that use exceptions, Go uses a simple and explicit method of returning error values. A function in Go often returns a value and an error. It's the caller's responsibility to check if the error is nil before proceeding.

Example:

```go
package main

import (
    "errors"
    "fmt"
)

// divide divides two integers and returns an error
if the divisor is zero.
func divide(a, b int) (int, error) {
    if b == 0 {
        return 0, errors.New("division by zero")
    }
    return a / b, nil
}

func main() {
    result, err := divide(10, 0)
    if err != nil {
        fmt.Println("Error:", err)
        return
    }
    fmt.Println("Result:", result)
}
```

Explanation:
The divide function returns an error if the divisor is zero. The caller checks if the error is nil before using the result. This explicit handling of errors forces the developer to address error cases rather than ignoring them.

2.1.2 Idiomatic Practices

Idiomatic Go encourages clear and concise error handling. Common practices include:

- **Returning Early:** Check for errors immediately and return if one occurs.

- **Wrapping Errors:** Use the fmt.Errorf function with the %w verb (introduced in Go 1.13) to wrap errors with additional context.

- **Sentinel Errors:** Define common error variables for frequently encountered errors.

- **Custom Error Types:** Create types that implement the error interface to provide more detailed context.

Example: Wrapping Errors

```go
package main

import (
    "fmt"
    "os"
)

func readFile(filename string) ([]byte, error) {
    data, err := os.ReadFile(filename)
    if err != nil {
        // Wrap the error with additional context.
        return nil, fmt.Errorf("readFile: unable to read %s: %w", filename, err)
    }
    return data, nil
}
```

```
func main() {
    _, err := readFile("nonexistent.txt")
    if err != nil {
        fmt.Println("Error:", err)
        return
    }
}
```

Explanation:

In this example, if os.ReadFile fails, the error is wrapped with additional context. This makes it easier to diagnose issues when errors propagate through your code.

2.1.3 Custom Error Types

Custom error types allow you to add context and structure to error messages. By defining your own error type, you can include additional fields and methods.

Example: Custom Error Type

```go
go

package main

import (
    "fmt"
)

// ValidationError represents an error with input
validation.
type ValidationError struct {
    Field   string
    Message string
}

func (ve *ValidationError) Error() string {
    return fmt.Sprintf("validation error on field
'%s': %s", ve.Field, ve.Message)
}

func validateInput(input string) error {
    if input == "" {
        return &ValidationError{
            Field:   "input",
```

```go
        Message: "input cannot be empty",
        }
    }
    return nil
}

func main() {
    err := validateInput("")
    if err != nil {
        fmt.Println("Error:", err)
        return
    }
    fmt.Println("Input is valid.")
}
```

Explanation:

Here, the ValidationError struct implements the error interface. It provides a detailed error message that can be used to identify which field failed validation and why.

2.2 Writing Tests in Go

Testing is a vital part of developing reliable software. Go comes with a built-in testing package that makes it straightforward to write and run tests.

2.2.1 Unit Testing

Unit tests verify that individual functions work as expected. A test file typically ends with _test.go, and test functions start with Test.

Example: Unit Test for Divide Function

```go
package main

import (
    "testing"
)

func TestDivide(t *testing.T) {
    result, err := divide(10, 2)
    if err != nil {
        t.Errorf("Expected no error, got %v", err)
    }
    if result != 5 {
```

```go
        t.Errorf("Expected result 5, got %d", result)
    }

    _, err = divide(10, 0)
    if err == nil {
        t.Errorf("Expected error for division by
zero, got nil")
    }
}
```

Explanation:
This test checks both a successful division and the error case. Using the testing package, you can use methods like t.Errorf to indicate test failures.

2.2.2 Integration Testing

Integration tests ensure that different parts of your application work together correctly. These tests can be more complex than unit tests and may involve interacting with databases, external services, or file systems.

Example: Integration Test for File Reading

```go
package main

import (
    "os"
    "testing"
)

func TestReadFileIntegration(t *testing.T) {
    // Create a temporary file with known content.
    tmpfile, err := os.CreateTemp("", "example")
    if err != nil {
        t.Fatal(err)
    }
    defer os.Remove(tmpfile.Name())

    content := []byte("Hello, World!")
    if _, err := tmpfile.Write(content); err != nil {
        t.Fatal(err)
    }
    tmpfile.Close()
```

```go
data, err := readFile(tmpfile.Name())
if err != nil {
    t.Errorf("Expected no error, got %v", err)
}
if string(data) != "Hello, World!" {
    t.Errorf("Expected content 'Hello, World!',
got %s", data)
}
}
```

Explanation:

This integration test creates a temporary file, writes known content, reads it using the readFile function, and verifies the output. Integration tests are crucial for verifying interactions between different components of your application.

2.2.3 Benchmarking

Benchmark tests measure the performance of your functions. They help you understand how your code scales under load.

Example: Benchmark for Divide Function

```go
go

package main

import "testing"

func BenchmarkDivide(b *testing.B) {
    for i := 0; i < b.N; i++ {
        _, _ = divide(100, 5)
    }
}
```

Explanation:

The benchmark function runs the divide function repeatedly to measure its performance. Run benchmarks using go test -bench=. to see the results.

2.2.4 Test Coverage

```
Test coverage tools help you determine which parts of
your code are exercised by tests. Run:
bash

go test -cover
```

This command provides a coverage percentage, helping you identify untested parts of your application.

---

3. Tools and Setup

Before writing tests and implementing robust error handling, ensure that your development environment is properly configured. This section outlines the essential tools and provides step-by-step instructions for setting up your Go workspace for error handling and testing.

3.1 Installing Go

1. **Download and Install:**
   Visit the Go downloads page and install the appropriate package for your operating system.

2. **Verify Installation:**
   Open your terminal and run:

```bash
```

```bash
go version
```
Confirm that the output shows the correct version of Go.

3.2 Configuring Your Workspace

Set up your Go workspace with the following directories:

- **src:** Your source code files.

- **pkg:** Compiled package objects.

- **bin:** Executable binaries.

Create your workspace:

```bash
```

```bash
mkdir -p $HOME/go/{src,pkg,bin}
Configure your environment by adding to your shell
configuration file (e.g., .bashrc):
bash
```

```bash
export GOPATH=$HOME/go
```

```
export PATH=$PATH:$GOPATH/bin
```
Then reload your configuration:

```
bash
```

```
source ~/.bashrc
```

3.3 IDE and Tools for Testing

- **IDE Setup:**
  Tools like Visual Studio Code and GoLand provide excellent support for testing with built-in features for running and debugging tests.

- **Go Test Command:**
  Use go test to run tests, and go test -bench=. to run benchmarks.

- **Coverage Tools:**
  The -cover flag in go test shows test coverage.

- **Version Control:**
  Use Git to manage your code and collaborate with other developers.

---

4. Hands-on Examples & Projects

This section provides practical projects and examples that bring together error handling and testing in Go. Each example is designed to build upon previous concepts, gradually increasing in complexity.

4.1 Project 1: Simple Calculator with Error Handling

Create a file named calculator.go:

```
go
```

```
package main

import (
    "fmt"
    "strconv"
    "errors"
```

```go
)

// calculate performs a basic arithmetic operation.
func calculate(aStr, bStr, op string) (int, error) {
    a, err := strconv.Atoi(aStr)
    if err != nil {
        return 0, fmt.Errorf("invalid number '%s': %w", aStr, err)
    }
    b, err := strconv.Atoi(bStr)
    if err != nil {
        return 0, fmt.Errorf("invalid number '%s': %w", bStr, err)
    }

    switch op {
    case "add":
        return a + b, nil
    case "subtract":
        return a - b, nil
    case "multiply":
        return a * b, nil
    case "divide":
        if b == 0 {
            return 0, errors.New("cannot divide by zero")
        }
        return a / b, nil
    default:
        return 0, fmt.Errorf("unsupported operation: %s", op)
    }
}

func main() {
    // Example usage: simulate user input.
    result, err := calculate("10", "2", "divide")
    if err != nil {
        fmt.Println("Error:", err)
        return
    }
    fmt.Println("Result:", result)
}
```

Explanation:
This project implements a simple calculator that takes two numbers (as strings) and an operation. It demonstrates proper error handling by validating inputs and wrapping errors with context.

4.2 Project 2: Testing the Calculator

Create a file named calculator_test.go:

```go

package main

import "testing"

func TestCalculate(t *testing.T) {
    // Test valid addition.
    result, err := calculate("5", "3", "add")
    if err != nil {
        t.Fatalf("Expected no error, got %v", err)
    }
    if result != 8 {
        t.Errorf("Expected result 8, got %d", result)
    }

    // Test division by zero.
    _, err = calculate("5", "0", "divide")
    if err == nil {
        t.Error("Expected error for division by zero, got nil")
    }

    // Test invalid operation.
    _, err = calculate("5", "3", "modulo")
    if err == nil {
        t.Error("Expected error for unsupported operation, got nil")
    }
}
```
Explanation:
This unit test verifies the functionality of the calculator. It checks for correct results, handles error conditions, and confirms that the appropriate error messages are returned.

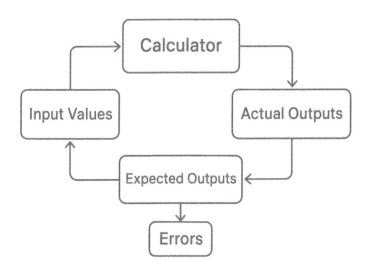

4.3 Project 3: Integration Testing with File I/O

Imagine you have a function that reads configurations from a file. Create a file named config.go:

```go
package main

import (
    "fmt"
    "os"
)

// loadConfig reads configuration data from a file.
func loadConfig(filename string) (string, error) {
    data, err := os.ReadFile(filename)
    if err != nil {
        return "", fmt.Errorf("loadConfig: failed to
read file %s: %w", filename, err)
    }
    return string(data), nil
}
```

```go
func main() {
    config, err := loadConfig("config.txt")
    if err != nil {
        fmt.Println("Error:", err)
        return
    }
    fmt.Println("Config Data:", config)
}
```

Now create an integration test in config_test.go:
go

```go
package main

import (
    "os"
    "testing"
)

func TestLoadConfigIntegration(t *testing.T) {
    // Create a temporary configuration file.
    tmpfile, err := os.CreateTemp("", "config_test")
    if err != nil {
        t.Fatal(err)
    }
    defer os.Remove(tmpfile.Name())

    content := "port=8080\nmode=production"
    if _, err := tmpfile.Write([]byte(content)); err != nil {
        t.Fatal(err)
    }
    tmpfile.Close()

    // Test loadConfig function.
    configData, err := loadConfig(tmpfile.Name())
    if err != nil {
        t.Errorf("Expected no error, got %v", err)
    }
    if configData != content {
        t.Errorf("Expected config data %q, got %q", content, configData)
    }
}
```

Explanation:
This integration test creates a temporary configuration file, writes known data to it, and then verifies that loadConfig returns the correct content. It demonstrates testing functions that interact with the file system.

4.4 Project 4: Benchmarking an Error-Prone Function

Create a file named benchmark_example_test.go:

```go

package main

import "testing"

func BenchmarkDivide(b *testing.B) {
    for i := 0; i < b.N; i++ {
        _, _ = divide(100, 5)
    }
}
```
Explanation:
This benchmark repeatedly calls the divide function to measure its performance. Benchmark tests help identify performance bottlenecks and optimize critical code paths.

5. Advanced Techniques & Optimization

In this section, we explore advanced strategies for error handling and testing, offering best practices and optimization tips for experienced developers.

5.1 Advanced Error Handling Strategies

5.1.1 Structured Logging and Error Context

As applications grow, simply printing error messages is often insufficient. Using structured logging (with libraries like logrus or zap) can help capture detailed context about errors.

Example: Using Structured Logging

```go
package main

import (
    "fmt"
    "github.com/sirupsen/logrus"
)

func process(data int) error {
    if data < 0 {
        return fmt.Errorf("invalid data: %d", data)
    }
    return nil
}

func main() {
    err := process(-10)
    if err != nil {
        logrus.WithFields(logrus.Fields{
            "module": "process",
            "data":    -10,
        }).Error("Error processing data:", err)
    }
}
```

Explanation:
This code uses structured logging to add context to an error, making it easier to diagnose issues in production.

5.1.2 Creating Rich Error Types

For complex systems, consider creating rich error types that include additional metadata, such as error codes or timestamps. This practice can improve error reporting and help automated tools categorize errors.

Example: Rich Error Type

```go
package main

import (
```

```go
    "fmt"
    "time"
)

type AppError struct {
    Code       int
    Message    string
    Timestamp  time.Time
}

func (e *AppError) Error() string {
    return fmt.Sprintf("[%d] %s at %s", e.Code,
e.Message, e.Timestamp.Format(time.RFC3339))
}

func performTask(success bool) error {
    if !success {
        return &AppError{
            Code:      500,
            Message:   "Task failed due to unknown
error",
            Timestamp: time.Now(),
        }
    }
    return nil
}

func main() {
    err := performTask(false)
    if err != nil {
        fmt.Println("Error:", err)
    }
}
```

Explanation:
The AppError struct adds extra information to error messages, which can be invaluable for debugging complex issues.

5.2 Advanced Testing Strategies

5.2.1 Table-Driven Tests

Table-driven tests allow you to write concise and scalable tests by specifying multiple test cases in a table format.

Example: Table-Driven Test for Divide Function

```go
package main

import "testing"

func TestDivideTableDriven(t *testing.T) {
    tests := []struct {
        a, b      int
        expected  int
        expectErr bool
    }{
        {10, 2, 5, false},
        {10, 0, 0, true},
        {15, 3, 5, false},
    }

    for _, tc := range tests {
        result, err := divide(tc.a, tc.b)
        if (err != nil) != tc.expectErr {
            t.Errorf("divide(%d, %d) unexpected error
state: %v", tc.a, tc.b, err)
        }
        if !tc.expectErr && result != tc.expected {
            t.Errorf("divide(%d, %d): expected %d,
got %d", tc.a, tc.b, tc.expected, result)
        }
    }
}
```

Explanation:

This test defines several cases in a slice of structs, iterates over them, and validates the results. It's an efficient way to cover multiple scenarios.

5.2.2 Mocking and Dependency Injection

For more complex systems, you might need to isolate components using mocks or dependency injection. While Go does not include a built-in mocking framework, you can create interfaces and write your own mocks.

Example: Using Interfaces for Testing

```go
```

```go
package main

import "fmt"

// DataFetcher defines an interface for fetching
data.
type DataFetcher interface {
    Fetch() (string, error)
}

// RealFetcher is a concrete implementation of
DataFetcher.
type RealFetcher struct{}

func (rf *RealFetcher) Fetch() (string, error) {
    return "real data", nil
}

// ProcessData processes data fetched by a
DataFetcher.
func ProcessData(df DataFetcher) (string, error) {
    data, err := df.Fetch()
    if err != nil {
        return "", err
    }
    return fmt.Sprintf("Processed: %s", data), nil
}

func main() {
    rf := &RealFetcher{}
    result, err := ProcessData(rf)
    if err != nil {
        fmt.Println("Error:", err)
        return
    }
    fmt.Println(result)
}
```

Explanation:
By defining the DataFetcher interface, you can later substitute a mock
implementation during testing.

5.3 Optimizing Test Performance

As your test suite grows, optimizing test performance becomes important. Strategies include:

- Running tests in parallel using t.Parallel().

- Isolating benchmarks from unit tests.

- Using caching for expensive setup operations.

Example: Running Tests in Parallel

go

```
func TestParallelExample(t *testing.T) {
    tests := []struct {
        input    int
        expected int
    }{
        {1, 1},
        {2, 4},
        {3, 9},
    }

    for _, tc := range tests {
        tc := tc // capture range variable
        t.Run(fmt.Sprintf("Input%d", tc.input),
func(t *testing.T) {
            t.Parallel()
            result := tc.input * tc.input
            if result != tc.expected {
                t.Errorf("Expected %d, got %d",
tc.expected, result)
            }
        })
    }
}
```

Explanation:

This example runs sub-tests in parallel, speeding up the overall test suite.

6. Troubleshooting and Problem-Solving

Even with best practices in place, you may encounter challenges when handling errors or writing tests. This section discusses common pitfalls and strategies for debugging and resolving issues.

6.1 Common Pitfalls in Error Handling

- **Ignoring Errors:**
  Failing to check for errors can lead to unexpected behavior. Always check returned error values.

- **Overly Verbose Errors:**
  While context is important, avoid cluttering error messages with unnecessary details.

- **Inconsistent Error Handling:**
  Ensure that error handling patterns are consistent across your codebase.

Before-and-After Example:
Before:

```go
result, _ := divide(10, 0)
// Error ignored; potential crash later.
After:
go

result, err := divide(10, 0)
if err != nil {
    fmt.Println("Error:", err)
    return
}
```

6.2 Troubleshooting Test Failures

- **Intermittent Failures:**
  These may be due to concurrency issues or uninitialized state. Use the -race flag and verbose logging to diagnose.

- **False Positives/Negatives:**
Ensure that your tests are deterministic. Table-driven tests can help standardize input/output comparisons.

- **Benchmark Inconsistencies:**
Run benchmarks multiple times to get reliable performance measurements.

6.3 Debugging Tools and Techniques

- **Logging:**
Use structured logging to capture additional context when errors occur.

- **IDE Debuggers:**
Leverage your IDE's debugging tools to set breakpoints, inspect variables, and step through code.

- **Code Reviews:**
Collaborate with peers to review error handling logic and test cases.

Before-and-After Example:
Before:
A test that fails without clear error messages.
After:
Enhanced logging that provides context about variable values and execution flow.

7. Conclusion & Next Steps

As we wrap up this chapter on error handling and testing, it's important to reflect on the key takeaways and consider how to apply these principles in your own projects.

Key Takeaways

- **Explicit Error Handling:**
Go's approach to error handling forces developers to consider error cases explicitly, resulting in more resilient code.

- **Idiomatic Practices:**
  Use early returns, wrap errors with context, and create custom error types to make debugging easier.

- **Testing Fundamentals:**
  Writing thorough unit tests, integration tests, and benchmarks helps ensure your code behaves as expected and performs efficiently.

- **Advanced Techniques:**
  Table-driven tests, structured logging, and dependency injection are powerful tools for building scalable and maintainable applications.

- **Continuous Improvement:**
  Integrating testing into your development workflow allows for continuous improvement and easier refactoring over time.

Reflecting on Your Learning

By integrating error handling and testing into your development process, you build a safety net that catches issues early and helps maintain code quality as your projects grow. The projects and examples provided in this chapter serve as a solid foundation for writing production-grade applications in Go. Every error you handle and every test you write not only improves your code but also deepens your understanding of robust software design.

Next Steps

- **Expand Your Test Suite:**
  As your application grows, add more tests to cover edge cases and unexpected scenarios.

- **Explore Advanced Testing Libraries:**
  Look into third-party libraries for mocking and behavior-driven development (BDD) to further enhance your testing capabilities.

- **Continuous Integration:**
  Integrate your tests into a CI/CD pipeline to ensure that your code is automatically tested before deployment.

- **Engage with the Community:**
  Participate in Go forums, contribute to open source projects, and share your testing and error-handling strategies with other developers.

Final Thoughts

Robust error handling and comprehensive testing are the cornerstones of high-quality software development. By embracing these practices, you not only reduce the likelihood of unexpected failures but also build confidence in your code's reliability and performance. Remember, every bug you fix and every test you write is a step toward mastering the art of programming in Go.

With the tools, techniques, and best practices outlined in this chapter, you are well-equipped to build, test, and maintain applications that can withstand real-world challenges. Keep experimenting, refining your approach, and integrating feedback from your testing efforts into your development process. Your journey toward becoming a proficient Go developer continues with every error handled and every test passed.

Chapter 6: Building Scalable Applications

1. Introduction

In today's fast-paced digital landscape, applications must be designed not only to work but to scale gracefully under increasing loads. Whether you're building a startup's first product or architecting an enterprise-level system, scalable application design is a critical factor for long-term success. This chapter introduces you to the architectural patterns, design principles, and security practices essential for building scalable, high-performance applications.

Why Scalability Matters

Scalability is the ability of a system to handle growth—in terms of data volume, user load, or functionality—without suffering performance degradation. A scalable application can efficiently manage spikes in traffic, distribute workloads, and recover from failures, ensuring continuous availability and a seamless user experience. Consider a popular social media platform: millions of users access it simultaneously, yet behind the scenes, the system distributes the workload across clusters of servers, implements load balancing, and uses microservices to keep every component independent and robust.

Key Concepts and Terminology

Before we delve into specific techniques, let's clarify some key terms:

- **Microservices:** An architectural style that structures an application as a collection of loosely coupled services. Each service implements a specific business capability.

- **RESTful API Design:** A design pattern for building web services that use HTTP methods to perform CRUD operations, ensuring statelessness and resource-oriented interactions.

- **Modular Coding Practices:** Techniques for dividing code into reusable, independent modules or packages that make applications easier to maintain and scale.

- **Load Balancing:** The process of distributing incoming network traffic across multiple servers to ensure no single server becomes a bottleneck.

- **Distributed Systems:** Systems in which components located on networked computers communicate and coordinate their actions by passing messages.

- **Secure Coding Practices:** Techniques for writing code that is resistant to common security threats such as injection attacks, data breaches, and unauthorized access.

Setting the Tone

Throughout this chapter, we will explore architectural patterns and best practices that empower you to build systems capable of handling exponential growth. We begin with microservices and RESTful API design as the foundation for modular and maintainable codebases. Then we move into scalability concerns such as load balancing and distributed systems, where practical strategies ensure high performance under pressure. Finally, we cover security considerations—an often overlooked but crucial component—by discussing secure coding practices and common pitfalls to avoid.

Visual Aid Suggestion:
Imagine a "roadmap" diagram that begins with a monolithic architecture on one side and gradually transitions to a distributed microservices-based architecture on the other. Along the route, icons represent load balancers, API gateways, and security shields, visually summarizing the journey from basic design to a full-fledged scalable system.

By the end of this chapter, you'll understand how to architect applications that are not only scalable and performant but also secure and resilient—traits essential for modern software development.

2. Core Concepts and Theory

This section provides detailed explanations of the core concepts behind building scalable applications. We cover architectural patterns, design principles for scalability, and security practices with real-world examples and analogies.

2.1 Architectural Patterns

Microservices

Microservices break down an application into small, independent services that communicate via lightweight protocols (often REST or messaging queues). This decoupling offers several benefits:

- **Independent Deployment:** Each service can be developed, deployed, and scaled independently.

- **Fault Isolation:** Failure in one service doesn't necessarily impact the entire system.

- **Technology Diversity:** Teams can choose the best technology stack for each service.

Analogy:
Imagine a fleet of food trucks instead of one large restaurant. Each truck specializes in a particular cuisine, and if one truck has an issue, the others continue serving customers.

Practical Example:

Consider an e-commerce application divided into services such as user management, product catalog, order processing, and payment handling. Each service exposes a **RESTful API**, allowing them to interact seamlessly while being independently deployable.

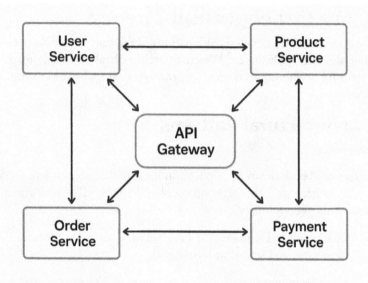

RESTful API Design

RESTful APIs use standard HTTP methods (GET, POST, PUT, DELETE) to interact with resources. Key principles include:

- **Statelessness:** Each request contains all the information needed for processing.

- **Resource-Oriented:** Use nouns for resources (e.g., /users, /orders) rather than actions.

- **Uniform Interface:** Simplifies interactions and makes it easier to understand and consume the API.

Real-World Example:
A blogging platform where clients can GET /posts to retrieve articles, POST /posts to create a new article, PUT /posts/{id} to update, and DELETE /posts/{id} to remove a post.

Practical Example:

Here's a simplified Go code snippet for a RESTful API endpoint:

```go
go

package main

import (
    "encoding/json"
    "log"
    "net/http"
)

// Post represents a blog post.
type Post struct {
    ID      int    `json:"id"`
    Title   string `json:"title"`
    Content string `json:"content"`
}

// posts slice to hold blog posts.
var posts = []Post{
    {ID: 1, Title: "Hello, World!", Content: "Welcome
to my blog."},
}

func getPosts(w http.ResponseWriter, r *http.Request)
{
    w.Header().Set("Content-Type",
"application/json")
    json.NewEncoder(w).Encode(posts)
}

func main() {
    http.HandleFunc("/posts", getPosts)
    log.Println("Server running on port 8080")
    log.Fatal(http.ListenAndServe(":8080", nil))
}
```

Modular Coding Practices

Modularity in coding means organizing your code into distinct, reusable components. This improves maintainability and scalability because modules can be developed and tested independently.

Best Practices Include:

- **Separation of Concerns:** Divide your code so that each module has a single responsibility.

- **Loose Coupling:** Modules interact through well-defined interfaces.

- **High Cohesion:** Related functionalities are kept together within the same module.

Analogy:
Think of building a house with prefabricated components: walls, windows, and doors are manufactured separately and then assembled. If one component needs repair, you can replace it without disturbing the rest of the structure.

2.2 Designing for Scalability

Designing for scalability involves planning for growth and ensuring that the system can handle increasing loads. Key concepts include:

Load Balancing

Load balancing distributes incoming traffic across multiple servers, ensuring that no single server becomes a bottleneck. Techniques include:

- **Round Robin:** Distributes requests evenly.

- **Least Connections:** Routes traffic to the server with the fewest active connections.

- **IP Hash:** Uses the client's IP address to consistently route traffic.

Real-World Example:
An online retailer during a holiday sale uses load balancing to handle the surge in web traffic by distributing requests across multiple instances.

Distributed Systems

Distributed systems split an application across multiple machines to improve availability, fault tolerance, and performance. Key concepts include:

- **Data Partitioning:** Dividing data across nodes.

- **Replication:** Maintaining copies of data to ensure availability.

- **Consistency:** Balancing between performance and data accuracy.

Real-World Example:
Google's Bigtable or Amazon's DynamoDB, which use distributed architectures to handle petabytes of data and millions of queries per second.

Best Practices for High Performance

- **Caching:** Use caching layers (like Redis or Memcached) to reduce load on primary data stores.

- **Asynchronous Processing:** Offload time-consuming tasks to background workers.

- **Horizontal Scaling:** Add more nodes to your system instead of increasing the power of individual nodes.

2.3 Security Considerations

When building scalable applications, security cannot be an afterthought. Secure coding practices help prevent vulnerabilities and protect sensitive data.

Secure Coding Practices

- **Input Validation:** Always validate and sanitize user inputs to prevent injection attacks.

- **Authentication and Authorization:** Use robust methods (e.g., OAuth, JWT) to secure endpoints.

- **Encryption:** Encrypt sensitive data both in transit and at rest.

- **Error Handling:** Avoid exposing sensitive information in error messages.

Real-World Example:
A financial application must ensure that all transactions are authenticated and that sensitive user data is encrypted to prevent breaches.

Common Pitfalls

- **Insecure Dependencies:** Regularly update libraries and dependencies to patch known vulnerabilities.

- **Poor Session Management:** Ensure sessions are securely handled and expired appropriately.

- **Misconfigured Servers:** Use security best practices for server configuration, including firewalls and secure communication protocols (HTTPS).

---

3. Tools and Setup

A robust development environment is crucial for building scalable applications. In this section, we outline the essential tools and provide step-by-step setup instructions to ensure you can implement the concepts covered in this chapter.

3.1 Essential Tools

- **Go Compiler and Runtime:**
  Download and install the latest version from the official Go website.

- **IDE/Text Editor:**
  Use Visual Studio Code, GoLand, or another editor with Go support to benefit from syntax highlighting, code completion, and integrated debugging.

- **Version Control:**
  Git is essential for managing source code and collaborating with teams.

- **Containerization:**
  Tools like Docker help package your applications for consistent deployment and scaling.

- **CI/CD Pipelines:**
  Jenkins, GitHub Actions, or GitLab CI can automate testing and deployment, ensuring continuous delivery.

3.2 Environment Setup

Installing Go

1. **Download:**
   Visit the Go downloads page and select the installer for your OS.

2. **Install:**
   Follow the installer instructions to set up Go on your system.

3. **Verify:**
   Open a terminal and run:

```bash
```

```
go version
```
Confirm that the correct version is displayed.

Configuring Your Workspace

Set up your Go workspace with these directories:

- **src:** For source code.

- **pkg:** For compiled packages.

- **bin:** For executables.

Create the workspace:

```bash
```

```
mkdir -p $HOME/go/{src,pkg,bin}
```
Add the following to your shell configuration file (e.g., .bashrc):

```bash
```

```
export GOPATH=$HOME/go
export PATH=$PATH:$GOPATH/bin
```
Reload your configuration:

```bash
```

```
source ~/.bashrc
```
Visual Aid Suggestion:

Setting Up an IDE

Using an IDE like Visual Studio Code enhances productivity:

1. **Install VS Code:**
   Download from Visual Studio Code's website.

2. **Install Go Extension:**
   Open the Extensions pane, search for "Go," and install the official extension.

3. **Configure the Extension:**
   Follow prompts to install supporting tools like gopls.

Additional Tools for Scaling and Security

- **Docker:**
  Install Docker to containerize your services, making them portable and easier to scale.

- **API Testing Tools:**
  Postman or Insomnia for testing RESTful APIs.

- **Security Scanners:**
  Tools such as OWASP ZAP or Snyk to scan for vulnerabilities.

---

4. Hands-on Examples & Projects

This section brings theory into practice with projects that incorporate architectural patterns, scalability design, and security best practices.

4.1 Project 1: Building a Microservices-Based Application

Overview

In this project, you'll build a simple e-commerce backend divided into microservices for user management, product catalog, and order processing. Each service will expose a RESTful API, and you'll implement modular coding practices to maintain separation of concerns.

Step-by-Step Walkthrough

1. **User Service:**
   Create a simple service for managing user data.

go

```go
// user_service.go
package main

import (
    "encoding/json"
    "log"
    "net/http"
)

type User struct {
    ID   int    `json:"id"`
    Name string `json:"name"`
}

var users = []User{
    {ID: 1, Name: "Alice"},
    {ID: 2, Name: "Bob"},
}

func getUsers(w http.ResponseWriter, r *http.Request)
{
    w.Header().Set("Content-Type",
"application/json")
    json.NewEncoder(w).Encode(users)
}

func main() {
    http.HandleFunc("/users", getUsers)
    log.Println("User service running on port 8081")
    log.Fatal(http.ListenAndServe(":8081", nil))
}
```

2. **Product Service:**
   Similarly, implement a service for products.

go

```go
// product_service.go
```

```go
package main

import (
    "encoding/json"
    "log"
    "net/http"
)

type Product struct {
    ID    int     `json:"id"`
    Name  string  `json:"name"`
    Price float64 `json:"price"`
}

var products = []Product{
    {ID: 101, Name: "Laptop", Price: 999.99},
    {ID: 102, Name: "Smartphone", Price: 499.99},
}

func getProducts(w http.ResponseWriter, r *http.Request) {
    w.Header().Set("Content-Type", "application/json")
    json.NewEncoder(w).Encode(products)
}

func main() {
    http.HandleFunc("/products", getProducts)
    log.Println("Product service running on port 8082")
    log.Fatal(http.ListenAndServe(":8082", nil))
}
```

3. **API Gateway:**
   Use an API gateway to route requests to the appropriate service.

```go
// gateway.go
package main

import (
    "io"
    "log"
    "net/http"
```

```
)

func proxyRequest(target string, w
http.ResponseWriter, r *http.Request) {
    resp, err := http.Get(target)
    if err != nil {
        http.Error(w, "Service unavailable",
http.StatusServiceUnavailable)
        return
    }
    defer resp.Body.Close()
    w.Header().Set("Content-Type",
"application/json")
    io.(w, resp.Body)
}

func main() {
    http.HandleFunc("/users", func(w
http.ResponseWriter, r *http.Request) {
        proxyRequest("http://localhost:8081/users",
w, r)
    })
    http.HandleFunc("/products", func(w
http.ResponseWriter, r *http.Request) {

proxyRequest("http://localhost:8082/products", w, r)
    })
    log.Println("API Gateway running on port 8080")
    log.Fatal(http.ListenAndServe(":8080", nil))
}
```

4.2 Project 2: Load Balancing and Distributed Design

Overview

This project simulates a distributed system by deploying multiple instances of a simple service behind a load balancer. For simplicity, you can use Docker Compose to run multiple containers.

Step-by-Step Walkthrough

1. **Dockerize a Service:**
   Create a Dockerfile for one of your services.

```
dockerfile

# Dockerfile for user service
FROM golang:1.18-alpine
WORKDIR /app
. .
RUN go build -o user_service .
CMD ["./user_service"]
```

2. **Docker Compose Setup:**

Create a docker-compose.yml file to run multiple instances.

```yaml
version: "3"
services:
  user1:
    build: ./user_service
    ports:
      - "8081:8081"
  user2:
    build: ./user_service
    ports:
      - "8083:8081"
  loadbalancer:
    image: nginx
    volumes:
      - ./nginx.conf:/etc/nginx/nginx.conf
    ports:
      - "80:80"
```

3. **NGINX Configuration for Load Balancing:**

```nginx
# nginx.conf
events { }
http {
    upstream user_service {
        server user1:8081;
        server user2:8081;
    }
    server {
        listen 80;
        location /users {
            proxy_pass http://user_service;
```

```
        }
      }
  }
```

4.3 Project 3: Secure RESTful API with Authentication

Overview

Enhance your RESTful API by adding security layers, including basic authentication and input validation. This example demonstrates secure coding practices integrated into a scalable API design.

Step-by-Step Walkthrough

    1.   **Secure Endpoint Implementation:**

```go
package main

import (
    "encoding/json"
    "log"
    "net/http"
)

type Message struct {
    Text string `json:"text"`
}

func secureEndpoint(w http.ResponseWriter, r
*http.Request) {
    username, password, ok := r.BasicAuth()
    if !ok || username != "admin" || password !=
"secret" {
        http.Error(w, "Unauthorized",
http.StatusUnauthorized)
        return
    }
    msg := Message{Text: "Secure content delivered."}
    w.Header().Set("Content-Type",
"application/json")
    json.NewEncoder(w).Encode(msg)
}

func main() {
    http.HandleFunc("/secure", secureEndpoint)
    log.Println("Secure API running on port 8090")
    log.Fatal(http.ListenAndServe(":8090", nil))
}
```

    2. **Input Validation:**
        Add robust input validation to ensure that all parameters are
        sanitized.

5. Advanced Techniques & Optimization

This section dives deeper into strategies that further enhance scalability, performance, and security in your applications.

5.1 Optimizing Architectural Patterns

- **Service Discovery:**
  Use tools like Consul or etcd for dynamic service discovery in a microservices architecture.

- **API Gateway Enhancements:**
  Implement rate limiting, caching, and circuit breakers to protect backend services.

- **Modularization:**
  Continuously refactor code into reusable packages, enforcing separation of concerns and loose coupling.

5.2 Performance Optimization Strategies

- **Caching Layers:**
  Integrate caching mechanisms (e.g., Redis) to reduce latency and load on databases.

- **Asynchronous Processing:**
  Offload heavy tasks to background workers using message queues (e.g., RabbitMQ, Kafka).

- **Horizontal Scaling:**
  Scale services by adding more instances rather than vertical scaling, which can be cost-prohibitive.

5.3 Advanced Security Considerations

- **Penetration Testing:**
  Regularly perform penetration tests to identify and remediate vulnerabilities.

- **Dependency Scanning:**
  Use tools to scan third-party libraries for known security issues.

- **Data Encryption:**
  Implement TLS for all communications and encrypt sensitive data at rest.

- **Secure Deployment:**
  Automate security checks in your CI/CD pipeline to prevent insecure code from reaching production.

Example: Secure Coding Tip

Always sanitize user inputs to prevent injection attacks:

```go
go

import "html/template"

// Example of sanitizing user input for safe HTML
output.
func safeOutput(input string) template.HTML {
    return
template.HTML(template.HTMLEscapeString(input))
}
```

5.4 Optimization Trade-offs

Discuss trade-offs such as:

- **Latency vs. Consistency:**
  In distributed systems, strong consistency may slow performance.

- **Security vs. Usability:**
  Overly strict security measures can hinder user experience.

- **Cost vs. Performance:**
  High-performance scaling can lead to increased infrastructure costs.

6. Troubleshooting and Problem-Solving

Even the best-designed scalable systems can face issues. This section offers strategies for troubleshooting common problems and debugging complex distributed systems.

6.1 Common Challenges

- **Service Failures:**
  When one microservice fails, ensure that fallback mechanisms or circuit breakers are in place.

- **Latency Issues:**
  Identify bottlenecks using profiling tools and adjust caching or load balancing strategies.

- **Security Breaches:**
  Implement logging and monitoring to detect unauthorized access or suspicious activities.

6.2 Debugging Techniques

- **Centralized Logging:**
  Use logging solutions like ELK stack or Prometheus with Grafana to monitor distributed systems.

- **Health Checks:**
  Implement endpoints for monitoring service health to detect failures early.

- **Simulated Load Testing:**
  Use tools like Apache JMeter or Locust to simulate high traffic and identify weak points.

Before-and-After Example:
Before: A monolithic error message with no context.
After: Structured logs with error codes and context that help pinpoint the issue.

6.3 Collaboration and Iteration

- **Peer Reviews:**
  Regular code and architecture reviews can uncover issues early.

- **Iterative Refactoring:**
  Continuously refactor components as your application scales and requirements evolve.

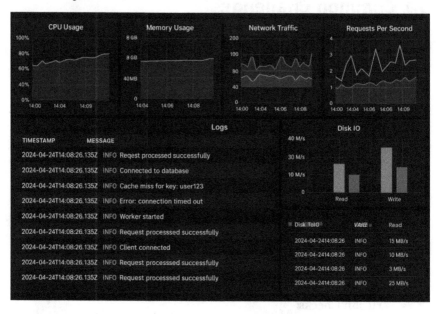

7. Conclusion & Next Steps

In this chapter, we explored the principles and practices behind building scalable applications—from architectural patterns such as microservices and RESTful API design to practical strategies for load balancing, distributed systems, and security. Let's summarize the key points and consider what comes next.

Key Takeaways

- **Architectural Patterns:**
  Embracing microservices and RESTful APIs allows for modular, independently scalable systems.

- **Designing for Scalability:**
  Load balancing, asynchronous processing, and horizontal scaling are critical techniques to handle increased loads.

- **Security Considerations:**
  Secure coding practices and proactive vulnerability management are integral to building robust systems.

- **Optimization Strategies:**
  Continuous monitoring, refactoring, and performance profiling ensure that your systems remain efficient as they scale.

Reflecting on Your Learning

Building scalable applications is not just about handling more traffic—it's about designing systems that are maintainable, secure, and resilient in the face of growth. The projects and examples provided in this chapter have illustrated real-world applications of these principles, from constructing microservices-based architectures to implementing robust API gateways and secure endpoints.

Next Steps

- **Deep Dive into Specific Areas:**
  Consider further study in areas like distributed databases, advanced load balancing algorithms, and cloud-native architectures.

- **Implement and Experiment:**
  Apply these concepts to your projects. Experiment with container orchestration tools like Kubernetes for automating scaling.

- **Continuous Learning:**
  Keep up-to-date with the latest trends in scalable architectures and security best practices by following industry blogs, attending conferences, and engaging with the developer community.

Final Thoughts

Scalability, performance, and security are the cornerstones of modern application design. As you continue on your journey, remember that every system—no matter how small at first—must be built with an eye toward growth and resilience. The strategies and best practices outlined in this chapter provide you with a roadmap to not only meet today's demands but also prepare for the challenges of tomorrow's rapidly evolving technological landscape.

Embrace these principles, experiment boldly, and never stop refining your approach. Your commitment to building scalable, secure, and high-performance applications will be the foundation upon which future innovations are built.

Chapter 7: Practical, Hands-On Projects

1. Introduction

In today's rapidly evolving software landscape, theory alone is not enough—practical, hands-on experience is essential to mastering a programming language and applying it to real-world scenarios. This chapter focuses on a series of projects that illustrate how to take the core concepts of Go and transform them into fully functional applications. Whether you are a beginner looking to see tangible results from your coding efforts, a professional aiming to build reliable and maintainable systems, or a hobbyist eager to experiment with new ideas, these projects are designed to equip you with actionable skills.

In this chapter, you will work through three distinct projects:

- **Project 1: Building a CLI Tool**
  Learn to create a command-line application with clear, step-by-step instructions. This project will introduce you to input parsing, output formatting, and error handling—all within the context of a practical tool you can run from your terminal.

- **Project 2: Developing a Web Server**
  Move into web development by creating a simple web server. You will learn about routing, handling HTTP requests, and serving responses in JSON format. This project highlights the use of Go's standard library for building web applications and demonstrates how to structure your code for clarity and maintainability.

- **Project 3: Microservices in Go**
  Take a deeper dive into building scalable systems by designing, coding, and deploying a microservice architecture. In this project, you will see how to break down an application into independent services, communicate via RESTful APIs, and use an API gateway to manage the system. Real-world scenarios such as user

management and product catalog services are used to illustrate the concepts.

Before you begin, let's define some key terminology and set the tone for the projects ahead:

- **CLI (Command-Line Interface):** A text-based user interface used to interact with software by typing commands.

- **Web Server:** A program that listens for HTTP requests and returns responses, usually in the form of web pages or data (such as JSON).

- **Microservices:** An architectural style where an application is structured as a collection of loosely coupled services, each responsible for a specific business capability.

- **RESTful API:** An interface that uses HTTP methods (GET, POST, PUT, DELETE) for communication between clients and servers, following the principles of Representational State Transfer (REST).

Throughout this chapter, our goal is to bridge the gap between theoretical knowledge and practical application. We provide clear instructions, detailed code examples, and visual aids to help you understand not only what to do, but why each step is important. Imagine you are constructing a building: the theories and concepts are your blueprints, while these projects are the actual construction process that turns those blueprints into a functional structure.

By the end of this chapter, you will have a portfolio of small, yet powerful applications that demonstrate your proficiency with Go. More importantly, you will have developed a deeper understanding of how to think about software design from a practical perspective—ready to tackle more complex challenges in your future projects.

2. Core Concepts and Theory

In this section, we explore the key concepts that underpin our projects. These core theories will not only guide your coding but also help you design applications that are modular, maintainable, and scalable.

2.1 Command-Line Tools and User Input

Command-line applications are among the simplest yet most powerful types of programs. They run in a terminal, take input from the user via arguments or standard input (stdin), and display output in text format. When designing a CLI tool, you should focus on:

- **Parsing Arguments:** Using packages such as flag to interpret command-line options.

- **Input Validation:** Ensuring that user inputs are valid before processing.

- **Output Formatting:** Presenting information in a clear, concise manner.

Real-World Analogy:
Consider a Swiss Army knife—compact, versatile, and ready for a variety of tasks. A well-designed CLI tool is similarly flexible and efficient, allowing users to quickly perform tasks without the overhead of a graphical user interface.

2.2 Building Web Servers

Web servers are the backbone of web applications. In Go, the net/http package provides all the tools necessary to create a robust web server. Key concepts include:

- **Routing:** Directing HTTP requests to the correct handler functions based on URL paths.

- **HTTP Methods:** Understanding GET, POST, PUT, DELETE, and how to use them appropriately.

- **JSON Encoding/Decoding:** Translating data between Go structures and JSON format, which is widely used for API communication.

- **Middleware:** Techniques for processing requests and responses, such as logging, authentication, and error handling.

Real-World Analogy:
Think of a web server as a restaurant. The routing system is like a maître d' who directs customers (requests) to the appropriate table (handler)

based on their needs. The kitchen (server logic) prepares the meal (response), and the wait staff (middleware) ensures the service is smooth and efficient.

2.3 Microservices and Service-Oriented Architectures

Microservices are an evolution of traditional monolithic architectures. Instead of a single codebase, an application is split into independent services that communicate over a network. The benefits include:

- **Scalability:** Each service can be scaled independently based on demand.

- **Resilience:** Failure in one service does not bring down the entire system.

- **Flexibility:** Different services can be implemented in different languages or frameworks, if needed.

In designing microservices, consider:

- **Service Boundaries:** Clearly define what each service is responsible for.

- **Communication Protocols:** Typically, RESTful APIs or messaging queues are used.

- **API Gateways:** A layer that aggregates multiple services and presents a unified interface to the client.

- **Data Consistency:** Strategies such as eventual consistency to handle data across distributed systems.

Real-World Analogy:
Imagine a large corporation where each department (e.g., HR, Finance, IT) operates independently yet collaborates to achieve the company's overall goals. Microservices work similarly, with each service focusing on a specific function while interacting with others to form a complete application.

2.4 Security, Scalability, and Maintainability

When building practical projects, security and scalability must be considered from the start. Key principles include:

- **Secure Coding:** Validate inputs, handle errors gracefully, and avoid exposing sensitive data.

- **Modular Design:** Write code in separate, self-contained modules that can be independently tested and scaled.

- **Documentation and Readability:** Clear documentation and well-commented code are essential for long-term maintenance and collaboration.

By grounding your projects in these core concepts, you'll be better prepared to build applications that not only work well but can evolve over time to meet new challenges.

3. Tools and Setup

Before diving into the projects, you need to have the right tools and environment in place. This section provides a detailed guide on setting up your development workspace for building Go applications.

3.1 Essential Tools and Software

- **Go Compiler and Runtime:**
  Download the latest version from the official Go website. This includes the compiler, runtime, and standard libraries.

- **Integrated Development Environment (IDE) or Text Editor:**
  We recommend using Visual Studio Code or GoLand. Both offer excellent support for Go, including code completion, debugging, and integrated testing tools.

- **Version Control:**
  Git is essential for tracking changes, collaborating with others, and managing your code repositories. Install Git from git-scm.com.

- **Containerization (Optional):**
  Docker is useful for packaging your applications and managing

dependencies in a consistent environment. It's especially beneficial when deploying microservices.

- **API Testing Tools:**
  Tools like Postman or Insomnia help you test web server endpoints and RESTful APIs.

- **Command-Line Tools:**
  Familiarize yourself with your system's terminal. Knowing basic shell commands is critical for building CLI tools and running Go programs.

3.2 Configuring Your Workspace

1. **Setting Up Your Go Workspace:**

Create a workspace directory with the following structure:

bash

```
mkdir -p $HOME/go/{src,pkg,bin}
```
Set the GOPATH environment variable by adding these lines to your shell configuration file (e.g., .bashrc or .zshrc):

bash

```
export GOPATH=$HOME/go
export PATH=$PATH:$GOPATH/bin
```
Reload your configuration:

bash

```
source ~/.bashrc
```

2. **Installing and Configuring an IDE:**

   o **Visual Studio Code:**

      1. Download and install VS Code from code.visualstudio.com.

      2. Open VS Code and navigate to the Extensions pane.

      3. Search for the "Go" extension and install the official extension.

> 4. Follow the prompts to install supporting tools such as gopls (Go language server) for enhanced code navigation and error checking.

3. **Setting Up Version Control:**

   o **Git Configuration:** Install Git and configure your username and email:

```bash
git config --global user.name "Your Name"
git config --global user.email
"youremail@example.com"
```

4. **Additional Tools:**

   o **Docker (Optional):** Install Docker from docker.com. Docker is useful for containerizing your microservices and ensuring a consistent deployment environment.

   o **Postman:** Download Postman from postman.com for testing your RESTful APIs.

By setting up your environment as described, you will be well-prepared to follow along with the hands-on projects in this chapter.

4. Hands-on Examples & Projects

This is the heart of the chapter—here we build practical applications that bring theory to life. We cover three projects, each progressively more complex and showcasing different aspects of Go programming.

Project 1: Building a CLI Tool

Overview

In this project, we'll build a command-line tool that allows users to manage a simple task list. The tool will enable adding, listing, and removing tasks from a to-do list. This project covers:

- Parsing command-line arguments.

- Reading user input.

- Managing state in memory.

- Outputting results in a clear, formatted way.

Step-by-Step Walkthrough

1. Creating the Project File:

Create a file named todo.go in your workspace:

```bash
cd $GOPATH/src
mkdir -p todoapp
cd todoapp
touch todo.go
```

2. Writing the Code:

```go
// todo.go
package main

import (
    "bufio"
    "fmt"
    "os"
    "strings"
)

// tasks holds the list of to-do items.
var tasks []string

// addTask appends a new task to the tasks slice.
func addTask(task string) {
    tasks = append(tasks, task)
    fmt.Println("Task added:", task)
}

// listTasks displays all current tasks.
func listTasks() {
    fmt.Println("Your To-Do List:")
    for i, task := range tasks {
        fmt.Printf("%d. %s\n", i+1, task)
    }
```

```go
}

// removeTask removes a task by index.
func removeTask(index int) {
    if index < 0 || index >= len(tasks) {
        fmt.Println("Invalid task number.")
        return
    }
    removed := tasks[index]
    tasks = append(tasks[:index], tasks[index+1:]...)
    fmt.Println("Task removed:", removed)
}

func main() {
    scanner := bufio.NewScanner(os.Stdin)
    for {
        fmt.Println("\nChoose an option: add, list,
remove, exit")
        scanner.Scan()
        input := strings.TrimSpace(scanner.Text())
        switch input {
        case "add":
            fmt.Print("Enter task: ")
            scanner.Scan()
            task := strings.TrimSpace(scanner.Text())
            addTask(task)
        case "list":
            listTasks()
        case "remove":
            fmt.Print("Enter task number to remove:
")
            scanner.Scan()
            var index int
            fmt.Sscanf(scanner.Text(), "%d", &index)
            removeTask(index - 1)
        case "exit":
            fmt.Println("Goodbye!")
            return
        default:
            fmt.Println("Unknown command. Please try
again.")
        }
    }
}
```

Explanation:
The CLI tool continuously prompts the user for commands. The user can add tasks, list current tasks, or remove a task by number. Input is read from the terminal using a scanner, and tasks are stored in a slice.

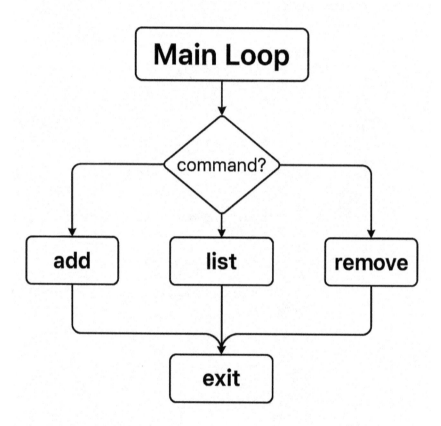

3. **Running the CLI Tool:**

Run the tool using:

```bash
```

```
go run todo.go
```
Follow the prompts to add, list, and remove tasks.

Project 2: Developing a Web Server

Overview

In this project, you will build a simple web server using Go's net/http package. The server will expose endpoints to serve data in JSON format. You'll learn about routing, handling HTTP requests, and using middleware for logging and error handling.

Step-by-Step Walkthrough

1. ### Creating the Project File:

Create a file named server.go:

```bash
cd $GOPATH/src
mkdir -p webserver
cd webserver
touch server.go
```

2. ### Writing the Code:

```go
// server.go
package main

import (
    "encoding/json"
    "log"
    "net/http"
)

// Message represents a simple message structure.
type Message struct {
    Greeting string `json:"greeting"`
}

// homeHandler handles requests to the root URL.
func homeHandler(w http.ResponseWriter, r
*http.Request) {
    w.Header().Set("Content-Type",
"application/json")
```

```
    msg := Message{Greeting: "Welcome to the Go Web
Server!"}
    json.NewEncoder(w).Encode(msg)
}

// aboutHandler handles requests to the /about URL.
func aboutHandler(w http.ResponseWriter, r
*http.Request) {
    w.Header().Set("Content-Type",
"application/json")
    msg := Message{Greeting: "This is a sample web
server built with Go."}
    json.NewEncoder(w).Encode(msg)
}

func main() {
    http.HandleFunc("/", homeHandler)
    http.HandleFunc("/about", aboutHandler)
    log.Println("Server is running on port 8080...")
    log.Fatal(http.ListenAndServe(":8080", nil))
}
```

Explanation:

This code creates a basic web server that responds with JSON data for the root (/) and /about endpoints. The http.HandleFunc function maps URL paths to handler functions.

3. **Testing the Web Server:**

Run the server:

```bash
bash
```

```
go run server.go
```
Open a browser and navigate to http://localhost:8080 and http://localhost:8080/about to see the responses.

Project 3: Microservices in Go
Overview

This project brings together many of the concepts from previous projects by building a simple microservice architecture. You'll design, code, and deploy multiple services that communicate over RESTful APIs, demonstrating how to create a modular, scalable system.

Step-by-Step Walkthrough

1. **Designing the Microservices:**

Our microservice architecture will consist of two services:

- o **User Service:** Manages user data.
- o **Product Service:** Manages product data.

Both services will expose RESTful endpoints, and an API gateway will route requests to the appropriate service.

2. **User Service Implementation:**

Create a file named user_service.go:

```go
// user_service.go
package main

import (
    "encoding/json"
    "log"
    "net/http"
)

// User represents a user in the system.
type User struct {
    ID    int    `json:"id"`
    Name  string `json:"name"`
}

var users = []User{
    {ID: 1, Name: "Alice"},
    {ID: 2, Name: "Bob"},
}

// getUsers handles GET requests for user data.
func getUsers(w http.ResponseWriter, r *http.Request)
{
```

```go
    w.Header().Set("Content-Type",
"application/json")
    json.NewEncoder(w).Encode(users)
}

func main() {
    http.HandleFunc("/users", getUsers)
    log.Println("User Service running on port
8081...")
    log.Fatal(http.ListenAndServe(":8081", nil))
}
```

3. **Product Service Implementation:**

Create a file named product_service.go:

```go
go

// product_service.go
package main

import (
    "encoding/json"
    "log"
    "net/http"
)

// Product represents a product in the catalog.
type Product struct {
    ID      int      `json:"id"`
    Name    string   `json:"name"`
    Price   float64  `json:"price"`
}

var products = []Product{
    {ID: 101, Name: "Laptop", Price: 999.99},
    {ID: 102, Name: "Smartphone", Price: 499.99},
}

// getProducts handles GET requests for product data.
func getProducts(w http.ResponseWriter, r
*http.Request) {
    w.Header().Set("Content-Type",
"application/json")
```

```go
        json.NewEncoder(w).Encode(products)
}

func main() {
    http.HandleFunc("/products", getProducts)
    log.Println("Product Service running on port
8082...")
    log.Fatal(http.ListenAndServe(":8082", nil))
}
```

4. API Gateway Implementation:

Create a file named api_gateway.go:

go

```go
// api_gateway.go
package main

import (
    "io"
    "log"
    "net/http"
)

// proxyRequest forwards requests to the target URL.
func proxyRequest(target string, w
http.ResponseWriter, r *http.Request) {
    resp, err := http.Get(target)
    if err != nil {
        http.Error(w, "Service Unavailable",
http.StatusServiceUnavailable)
        return
    }
    defer resp.Body.Close()
    w.Header().Set("Content-Type",
"application/json")
    io.(w, resp.Body)
}

func main() {
    http.HandleFunc("/users", func(w
http.ResponseWriter, r *http.Request) {
        proxyRequest("http://localhost:8081/users",
w, r)
```

```
    })
    http.HandleFunc("/products", func(w
http.ResponseWriter, r *http.Request) {

proxyRequest("http://localhost:8082/products", w, r)
    })
    log.Println("API Gateway running on port
8080...")
    log.Fatal(http.ListenAndServe(":8080", nil))
}
```

Explanation:
The API gateway routes requests to /users and /products by proxying them to the corresponding microservices running on different ports.

5. Deploying the Microservices:

For a production-like scenario, consider containerizing each service using Docker and orchestrating them with Docker Compose or Kubernetes. This modular setup ensures that services can scale independently and be updated without affecting the entire system.

Optional Docker Setup:
Create separate Dockerfiles for each service, then use a docker-compose.yml file to run them together.

---

5. Advanced Techniques & Optimization

In this section, we explore strategies for improving the performance, scalability, and maintainability of your projects. These techniques are geared toward experienced developers looking to optimize their implementations further.

5.1 Enhancing CLI Tools

- **Input/Output Improvements:**
  Use libraries for richer text formatting (such as spf13/cobra for CLI commands).

- **Modularity:**
  Organize your code into packages. For example, separate task management logic from input/output handling.

- **Testing:**
  Write unit tests for your CLI functions and use mock inputs to simulate user interactions.

5.2 Optimizing Web Servers

- **Middleware:**
  Implement middleware for logging, authentication, and error handling. This helps separate concerns and improves code readability.

- **Concurrency:**
  Use goroutines to handle long-running requests or background tasks, ensuring your server remains responsive under load.

- **Caching:**
  Incorporate caching mechanisms (e.g., in-memory caching with groupcache) to reduce response times.

5.3 Microservices Best Practices

- **Service Discovery and Load Balancing:**
  Use tools like Consul, etcd, or Kubernetes' built-in service discovery to dynamically route traffic to available service instances.

- **API Gateway Enhancements:**
  Enhance your gateway with rate limiting, circuit breakers, and caching to prevent overloading backend services.

- **Logging and Monitoring:**
  Integrate centralized logging (using ELK stack or Prometheus with Grafana) to monitor service health and performance.

- **Security:**
  Secure inter-service communication with TLS and use JWT or OAuth for authentication.

6. Troubleshooting and Problem-Solving

Even well-designed projects encounter issues. In this section, we discuss common challenges and strategies for troubleshooting and resolving problems in your projects.

6.1 Common Pitfalls

- **CLI Tool:**

    o **Incorrect Input Handling:** Validate all user inputs to avoid crashes.

    o **Poor Error Messages:** Ensure errors are informative and guide the user on what to fix.

- **Web Server:**

    o **Routing Issues:** Double-check your URL mappings and handler functions.

    o **Concurrency Bottlenecks:** Use profiling tools to identify slow handlers.

- **Microservices:**

    o **Service Unavailability:** Implement health checks and fallback mechanisms in your API gateway.

    o **Network Latency:** Use asynchronous processing where possible and optimize data serialization.

6.2 Debugging Techniques

- **Logging:**
  Use detailed logging (consider structured logging) to trace request flows and errors.

- **Breakpoints and IDE Debuggers:**
  Leverage your IDE's debugging tools to inspect variables and step through your code.

- **Testing with Mocks:**
  For microservices, use mock services during testing to isolate failures.

- **Profiling:**
  Use Go's pprof package to analyze performance bottlenecks.

Before-and-After Example:
Before: A microservice fails silently under load.
After: Logging and monitoring reveal that a particular endpoint is causing delays, leading to targeted optimization.

---

7. Conclusion & Next Steps

As we conclude this chapter, let's summarize the key points and outline how you can continue building on what you've learned.

Key Takeaways

- **Practical Application:**
  Hands-on projects provide an effective way to learn by doing. The CLI tool, web server, and microservice projects demonstrate how core concepts translate into real-world applications.

- **Modular and Scalable Design:**
  Building applications with a focus on modularity and scalability is critical. Whether through simple command-line tools or distributed microservices, designing for growth is essential.

- **Security and Performance:**
  Every project must consider security best practices and performance optimizations. Even small projects benefit from thoughtful error handling, logging, and efficient resource management.

- **Iterative Improvement:**
  The journey from a basic prototype to a production-ready system is iterative. Continuous testing, debugging, and refactoring are vital for long-term success.

Reflecting on Your Learning

These projects illustrate the entire development cycle—from setting up your environment and writing code, to deploying a scalable microservice architecture. By working through these hands-on examples, you gain practical experience that reinforces theoretical knowledge. This chapter is designed to be a launchpad; every project is an opportunity to refine your approach, learn new techniques, and prepare for more complex challenges.

Next Steps

- **Expand Your Projects:**
  Enhance the CLI tool with additional features, such as persistent storage or more sophisticated command parsing.

- **Integrate Advanced Middleware:**
  For the web server, consider adding middleware for authentication, logging, and request throttling.

- **Deploy to Production:**
  Experiment with container orchestration tools such as Kubernetes to deploy and manage your microservices at scale.

- **Continuous Integration and Testing:**
  Integrate your projects with CI/CD pipelines to automate testing and deployment. Explore automated testing frameworks and code coverage tools.

- **Learn and Collaborate:**
  Engage with the Go community, contribute to open source projects, and share your experiences to learn from others.

Final Thoughts

Practical, hands-on projects are the bridge between learning and doing. By building a CLI tool, a web server, and a microservice architecture, you have seen firsthand how the principles of modular design, scalability, and security come together to create real-world applications. These projects are more than exercises—they are the foundation upon which you can build increasingly complex and robust systems.

As you move forward, keep experimenting, keep testing, and never stop learning. Every line of code you write is an opportunity to innovate and improve. Embrace the challenges of building scalable applications, and use the knowledge gained in this chapter as a stepping stone toward mastering the art of software development.

Happy coding, and may your projects continue to grow, scale, and evolve with every new challenge you conquer!

Chapter 8: Advanced Topics

In modern software development, mastering advanced topics is essential to building robust, high-performance applications. In this chapter, we delve deep into the advanced aspects of Go programming. We cover performance tuning—including profiling, debugging, and optimization techniques; network programming with TCP/UDP communications and Go's networking libraries; and advanced concurrency with synchronization techniques and patterns drawn from real-world case studies. Whether you're a beginner looking to advance your skills, a professional seeking optimization strategies, or a hobbyist curious about the intricacies of Go, this chapter provides an in-depth exploration of the topics that make your applications faster, more efficient, and scalable.

---

1. Introduction

Modern applications are expected to be fast, scalable, and reliable under heavy load. As you develop complex systems, performance bottlenecks, network latency, and concurrent operations become major challenges that can affect the overall user experience and operational costs. This chapter focuses on advanced topics in Go that are vital for overcoming these challenges.

The Importance of Advanced Topics

Performance tuning is not merely about making code run faster—it's about creating applications that can scale seamlessly as the demands on them increase. Debugging and profiling are critical tools for identifying bottlenecks and inefficiencies, while optimization techniques ensure that your application uses resources efficiently.

Network programming is another cornerstone of modern software development. Today's applications frequently communicate over networks, requiring robust mechanisms for managing TCP and UDP connections, handling high volumes of concurrent requests, and ensuring secure data transfer. Go's built-in networking libraries simplify these tasks, enabling you to build networked applications that are both powerful and easy to maintain.

Advanced concurrency is the third pillar we explore. Concurrency in Go goes far beyond launching goroutines; it involves mastering synchronization techniques, advanced concurrency patterns, and real-world strategies to avoid pitfalls like race conditions and deadlocks. These advanced topics enable you to harness the full potential of multi-core processors and build applications that perform reliably under high loads.

Key Concepts and Terminology

Before diving in, let's define some key terms:

- **Profiling:** The process of measuring various aspects of program performance (e.g., CPU and memory usage) to identify bottlenecks.

- **Debugging:** Systematically locating and fixing bugs or issues within your code.

- **Optimization:** Techniques used to improve performance, often by reducing resource usage or execution time.

- **TCP/UDP:** Protocols used for network communication. TCP (Transmission Control Protocol) ensures reliable, ordered data delivery, while UDP (User Datagram Protocol) is faster but less reliable.

- **Synchronization:** Mechanisms to coordinate the execution of concurrently running operations, ensuring correct results.

- **Concurrency Patterns:** Reusable solutions for common problems in concurrent programming (e.g., worker pools, fan-out/fan-in).

Setting the Tone

This chapter is designed to be both comprehensive and accessible. We'll start with a solid foundation in theory and gradually build up to hands-on projects that allow you to apply these advanced topics in real-world scenarios. Visual aids—such as diagrams of data flows and system architectures—will be suggested throughout to help clarify complex concepts. Whether you are optimizing a microservice, building a high-throughput network server, or fine-tuning concurrent operations, you'll find actionable insights that empower you to create high-performance Go applications.

Imagine your application as a high-performance sports car. The engine tuning (profiling and optimization), advanced navigation systems (network programming), and coordinated team effort (advanced concurrency) are all essential for the car to perform at its best. By mastering these advanced topics, you ensure that your software runs as smoothly and efficiently as a finely tuned machine.

---

2. Core Concepts and Theory

In this section, we explore the theoretical underpinnings of performance tuning, network programming, and advanced concurrency in Go. Each subsection provides detailed explanations, real-world analogies, and examples that illustrate how these concepts come together to form the backbone of high-performance applications.

2.1 Performance Tuning

2.1.1 Profiling in Go

Profiling is the systematic process of analyzing your application to determine where time and resources are being consumed. Go offers a robust built-in profiling tool called pprof that helps you visualize CPU usage, memory allocation, and goroutine activity.

Key Concepts:

- **CPU Profiling:** Identifies functions or processes that consume excessive CPU cycles.

- **Memory Profiling:** Helps pinpoint memory leaks or inefficient memory use.

- **Goroutine Profiling:** Reveals how goroutines are spawned and whether any are leaking or causing contention.

Real-World Analogy:
Imagine a factory where you want to maximize productivity. Profiling is like a time-motion study that identifies bottlenecks on the assembly line. Once you know where the delays occur, you can optimize the workflow.

Example: CPU Profiling Setup

```go
package main

import (
    "log"
    "os"
    "runtime/pprof"
    "time"
)

func intensiveTask() {
    time.Sleep(100 * time.Millisecond) // Simulate a
CPU-bound task
}

func main() {
    // Create a CPU profile file
    f, err := os.Create("cpu.prof")
    if err != nil {
        log.Fatal("could not create CPU profile: ",
err)
    }
    defer f.Close()

    // Start CPU profiling
    if err := pprof.StartCPUProfile(f); err != nil {
        log.Fatal("could not start CPU profile: ",
err)
    }
    defer pprof.StopCPUProfile()

    for i := 0; i < 1000; i++ {
        intensiveTask()
    }
    log.Println("CPU profiling complete")
}
```

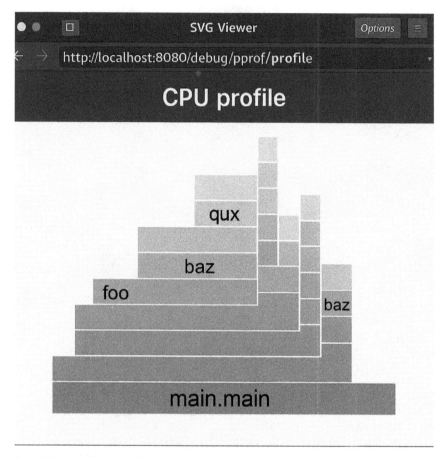

2.1.2 Debugging and Optimization

Debugging is critical for ensuring that your application behaves as expected, especially when optimizing for performance. Go's tooling and its simple error handling model make it easier to track down issues.

Strategies for Effective Debugging:

- **Verbose Logging:** Insert detailed log statements to trace execution flow.

- **Interactive Debuggers:** Use IDEs like GoLand or VS Code with integrated debugging tools.

- **Race Detector:** Run your program with the -race flag to catch race conditions early.

Example: Debugging with Verbose Logging

```go
package main

import (
    "log"
    "time"
)

func processItem(id int) {
    log.Printf("Processing item %d started", id)
    time.Sleep(50 * time.Millisecond)
    log.Printf("Processing item %d finished", id)
}

func main() {
    for i := 1; i <= 10; i++ {
        go processItem(i)
    }
    time.Sleep(1 * time.Second)
}
```

Explanation:

This code logs the start and end of processing for each item, allowing you to trace the execution order and identify slow operations.

2.1.3 Optimizing Code for Speed and Efficiency

Optimization involves rewriting code to reduce execution time and resource usage. Best practices include:

- **Minimizing Allocations:** Use slices with preallocated capacity to reduce memory reallocations.

- **Inlining Functions:** Let the compiler inline small functions for faster execution.

- **Efficient Data Structures:** Choose data structures that best fit your use case (e.g., maps vs. slices).

Real-World Example:
Consider an image processing application that handles large datasets. Optimizing the code to reduce memory allocations can significantly speed up processing and reduce latency.

Example: Optimizing Slice Usage

go

```go
func processData(data []int) []int {
    // Preallocate the results slice with the same
capacity as input data.
    results := make([]int, 0, len(data))
    for _, v := range data {
        results = append(results, v*2)
    }
    return results
}
```

2.2 Network Programming

Network programming is essential for building distributed applications. Go's standard library provides a rich set of tools for TCP/UDP communication and HTTP server/client implementations.

2.2.1 TCP and UDP Communication

TCP (Transmission Control Protocol):
TCP is used for reliable, connection-oriented communication. It ensures that data is delivered in order and without loss.

UDP (User Datagram Protocol):
UDP is connectionless and does not guarantee delivery, making it faster but less reliable. It is used for applications where speed is critical and occasional data loss is acceptable (e.g., live video streaming).

Example: TCP Server in Go

go

```go
package main

import (
    "bufio"
    "fmt"
```

```go
    "net"
)

func main() {
    listener, err := net.Listen("tcp", ":8080")
    if err != nil {
        fmt.Println("Error starting TCP server:",
err)
        return
    }
    defer listener.Close()
    fmt.Println("TCP server listening on port 8080")

    for {
        conn, err := listener.Accept()
        if err != nil {
            fmt.Println("Error accepting
connection:", err)
            continue
        }
        go handleConnection(conn)
    }
}

func handleConnection(conn net.Conn) {
    defer conn.Close()
    reader := bufio.NewReader(conn)
    for {
        message, err := reader.ReadString('\n')
        if err != nil {
            break
        }
        fmt.Print("Received:", message)
        conn.Write([]byte("Echo: " + message))
    }
}
```

Explanation:

This TCP server listens for connections on port 8080 and echoes back any messages received. Each connection is handled in a separate goroutine to allow concurrent handling of multiple clients.

Example: UDP Server in Go

```go
go

package main

import (
    "fmt"
    "net"
)

func main() {
    addr, err := net.ResolveUDPAddr("udp", ":8081")
    if err != nil {
        fmt.Println("Error resolving address:", err)
        return
    }
    conn, err := net.ListenUDP("udp", addr)
    if err != nil {
        fmt.Println("Error listening on UDP port:",
err)
        return
    }
    defer conn.Close()
    fmt.Println("UDP server listening on port 8081")

    buffer := make([]byte, 1024)
    for {
        n, addr, err := conn.ReadFromUDP(buffer)
        if err != nil {
            fmt.Println("Error reading UDP packet:",
err)
            continue
        }
        fmt.Printf("Received from %v: %s\n", addr,
string(buffer[:n]))
        conn.WriteToUDP([]byte("Echo:
"+string(buffer[:n])), addr)
    }
}
```

2.2.2 Building Networked Applications

Using Go's networking libraries, you can build complex networked applications like chat servers, file transfer utilities, or real-time data processors.

Example: Simple Chat Server (Outline)

- **Clients Connect:** Clients establish TCP connections.

- **Message Broadcasting:** The server receives messages and broadcasts them to all connected clients.

- **Concurrency:** Each client is handled in its own goroutine for real-time communication.

2.3 Advanced Concurrency

Advanced concurrency involves using synchronization techniques and patterns to manage complex, concurrent systems.

2.3.1 Synchronization Techniques

Mutexes:
A mutex is a locking mechanism to ensure that only one goroutine accesses a critical section of code at a time.

Example: Using a Mutex

```go
go

package main

import (
    "fmt"
    "sync"
)

var (
    counter int
    mu       sync.Mutex
)

func increment() {
    mu.Lock()
```

```
    counter++
    mu.Unlock()
}

func main() {
    var wg sync.WaitGroup
    for i := 0; i < 1000; i++ {
        wg.Add(1)
        go func() {
            defer wg.Done()
            increment()
        }()
    }
    wg.Wait()
    fmt.Println("Counter:", counter)
}
```

Explanation:

This code uses a mutex to protect the shared variable counter from concurrent access issues.

Channels for Synchronization:

Channels can be used not only for communication but also for synchronizing goroutines.

2.3.2 Advanced Concurrency Patterns

Worker Pools:

We discussed worker pools in earlier chapters. In advanced systems, worker pools manage large volumes of tasks while controlling resource usage.

Fan-Out / Fan-In:

This pattern distributes work across multiple goroutines (fan-out) and then collects the results (fan-in) for aggregation.

Real-World Case Study:

Consider a web crawler that distributes URL fetching tasks among multiple workers. The results are then combined to create a complete index of web pages.

Example: Fan-Out / Fan-In Pattern (Simplified)

```go
go

package main

import (
    "fmt"
    "sync"
    "time"
)

func fetchURL(url string, ch chan<- string, wg
*sync.WaitGroup) {
    defer wg.Done()
    // Simulate fetching URL
    time.Sleep(100 * time.Millisecond)
    ch <- fmt.Sprintf("Content from %s", url)
}

func main() {
    urls := []string{"http://example.com",
"http://golang.org", "http://github.com"}
    results := make(chan string, len(urls))
    var wg sync.WaitGroup

    for _, url := range urls {
        wg.Add(1)
        go fetchURL(url, results, &wg)
    }
    go func() {
        wg.Wait()
        close(results)
    }()

    for res := range results {
        fmt.Println(res)
    }
}
```

2.3.3 Real-World Concurrency Case Studies

- **High-Frequency Trading Platforms:**
  Use advanced concurrency to handle real-time data streams and execute trades in milliseconds.

- **Streaming Services:**
  Manage concurrent data streams to deliver high-quality video or audio content.

- **Distributed Logging Systems:**
  Aggregate logs from multiple sources concurrently for real-time monitoring and analytics.

Case Study
High-Frequency Trading System

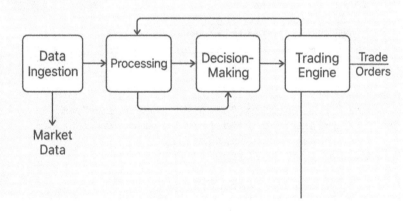

---

3. Tools and Setup

Before exploring hands-on projects, ensure your environment is optimized for advanced topics. In this section, we detail the tools and setup necessary for performance tuning, network programming, and advanced concurrency.

3.1 Essential Tools

- **Go Compiler and Runtime:**
  Install the latest version from golang.org/dl.

- **IDE or Text Editor:**
  Visual Studio Code, GoLand, or Sublime Text with Go plugins are recommended.

- **Profiling Tools:**
  Use Go's built-in pprof tool for profiling. External tools like Grafana or Prometheus can enhance monitoring.

- **Network Debugging Tools:**
  Wireshark for packet analysis, Postman for testing APIs.

- **Version Control:**
  Git for managing code and collaboration.

- **Docker:**
  Containerize your applications to ensure consistent environments across development and production.

- **CI/CD Pipelines:**
  Jenkins, GitHub Actions, or GitLab CI for automated testing and deployment.

3.2 Setting Up Your Development Environment

1. **Configure Your Go Workspace:**

```bash
mkdir -p $HOME/go/{src,pkg,bin}
export GOPATH=$HOME/go
export PATH=$PATH:$GOPATH/bin
source ~/.bashrc
```

2. **IDE Configuration:**

   o Install and configure Visual Studio Code with the Go extension.

   o Set up debugging and profiling configurations. *Visual Aid:* Screenshot of VS Code with Go extension and debugging panels.

3. **Docker Setup (Optional):**

- o Install Docker and Docker Compose to containerize advanced projects. *Visual Aid:* Diagram of a containerized microservices architecture.

4. **Additional Setup:**

- o Install Wireshark and Postman for network debugging.

- o Configure Git for version control.

- o Set up a CI/CD pipeline for automated testing. *Visual Aid:* Flowchart showing a CI/CD pipeline from code commit to deployment.

---

4. Hands-on Examples & Projects

This section provides detailed, practical projects that demonstrate advanced topics in action. Each project builds on previous concepts and incorporates performance tuning, network programming, and advanced concurrency.

Project 1: Performance Tuning a Data Processing Application

Overview

In this project, you will optimize a data processing application to run faster and more efficiently. You'll integrate profiling, optimize memory usage, and debug performance bottlenecks.

Step-by-Step Walkthrough

1. **Initial Implementation:** Create a file named dataprocessor.go:

```go
package main

import (
    "fmt"
    "time"
)
```

```go
// process simulates a CPU-intensive task.
func process(data []int) []int {
    results := make([]int, len(data))
    for i, v := range data {
        time.Sleep(10 * time.Millisecond) // Simulate
delay
        results[i] = v * v
    }
    return results
}

func main() {
    data := []int{1, 2, 3, 4, 5, 6, 7, 8, 9, 10}
    start := time.Now()
    results := process(data)
    duration := time.Since(start)
    fmt.Println("Results:", results)
    fmt.Println("Processing Time:", duration)
}
```

Explanation:

This program processes an array of integers by squaring each element. A sleep delay simulates CPU work.

2. **Profiling the Application:** Integrate CPU profiling using pprof as shown in previous sections.

go

```go
// Add profiling setup in main()
import (
    "os"
    "runtime/pprof"
    "log"
)

func main() {
    f, err := os.Create("cpu.prof")
    if err != nil {
        log.Fatal(err)
    }
    defer f.Close()
    pprof.StartCPUProfile(f)
    defer pprof.StopCPUProfile()
```

```
// ... rest of the code
}
```

3. **Optimizing the Code:**

   o   Reduce sleep durations.

   o   Preallocate slices efficiently.

   o   Refactor code for better performance. *Before-and-After Example:*
       Show the original processing loop versus an optimized version.

4. **Benchmarking:** Write a benchmark test in dataprocessor_test.go:

```go
package main

import "testing"

func BenchmarkProcess(b *testing.B) {
    data := []int{1, 2, 3, 4, 5, 6, 7, 8, 9, 10}
    for i := 0; i < b.N; i++ {
        _ = process(data)
    }
}
```

Project 2: Building an Advanced Network Application

Overview

This project involves creating a networked application that handles TCP and UDP communications. You'll build a TCP echo server and a UDP broadcaster, integrating both into a single application to demonstrate versatile network programming.

Step-by-Step Walkthrough

1. **TCP Echo Server:** Create a file named tcp_server.go:

```go
package main
```

```go
import (
    "bufio"
    "fmt"
    "net"
)

func handleTCPConnection(conn net.Conn) {
    defer conn.Close()
    reader := bufio.NewReader(conn)
    for {
        message, err := reader.ReadString('\n')
        if err != nil {
            break
        }
        fmt.Printf("Received: %s", message)
        conn.Write([]byte("Echo: " + message))
    }
}

func main() {
    listener, err := net.Listen("tcp", ":9090")
    if err != nil {
        fmt.Println("TCP server error:", err)
        return
    }
    defer listener.Close()
    fmt.Println("TCP server listening on port 9090")
    for {
        conn, err := listener.Accept()
        if err != nil {
            fmt.Println("Error accepting
connection:", err)
            continue
        }
        go handleTCPConnection(conn)
    }
}
```

Explanation:
The TCP server listens on port 9090 and echoes back any messages it receives.

2. **UDP Broadcaster:** Create a file named udp_broadcaster.go:

```go
go

package main

import (
    "fmt"
    "net"
    "time"
)

func main() {
    addr, err := net.ResolveUDPAddr("udp",
"255.255.255.255:9091")
    if err != nil {
        fmt.Println("Error resolving address:", err)
        return
    }
    conn, err := net.DialUDP("udp", nil, addr)
    if err != nil {
        fmt.Println("Error dialing UDP:", err)
        return
    }
    defer conn.Close()

    for {
        message := []byte("Hello, UDP network!\n")
        _, err := conn.Write(message)
        if err != nil {
            fmt.Println("Error sending message:",
err)
        }
        time.Sleep(2 * time.Second)
    }
}
```

Explanation:
This UDP broadcaster sends a message every two seconds to a broadcast address.

3. **Integrating TCP and UDP:** Develop a combined application that launches both the TCP server and UDP broadcaster concurrently using goroutines. *Visual Aid:*
   A system diagram showing the TCP server and UDP broadcaster

as parallel components, with clients connecting to TCP and receiving UDP broadcasts.

Project 3: Advanced Microservices with Concurrency

Overview

In this project, you'll design and deploy a microservice architecture that leverages advanced concurrency patterns. This includes using worker pools, fan-out/fan-in patterns, and synchronizing multiple services to build a resilient system.

Step-by-Step Walkthrough

1. **Designing the Architecture:** Plan a simple system with three services:

   o **Order Service:** Receives orders.

   o **Inventory Service:** Manages product stocks.

   o **Notification Service:** Sends notifications upon order completion.

An API gateway routes requests to the appropriate services.

2. **Implementing the Order Service:** Create a file named order_service.go:

```go
package main

import (
    "encoding/json"
    "log"
    "net/http"
)

type Order struct {
    ID       int    `json:"id"`
    Product  string `json:"product"`
    Quantity int    `json:"quantity"`
}
```

```go
var orders []Order

func createOrder(w http.ResponseWriter, r
*http.Request) {
    var order Order
    err := json.NewDecoder(r.Body).Decode(&order)
    if err != nil {
        http.Error(w, "Invalid order data",
http.StatusBadRequest)
        return
    }
    orders = append(orders, order)
    w.Header().Set("Content-Type",
"application/json")
    json.NewEncoder(w).Encode(order)
    // Simulate asynchronous notification
    go sendNotification(order)
}

func sendNotification(order Order) {
    // This function would normally integrate with
Notification Service
    log.Printf("Notification sent for Order ID %d",
order.ID)
}

func main() {
    http.HandleFunc("/orders", createOrder)
    log.Println("Order Service running on port
8083...")
    log.Fatal(http.ListenAndServe(":8083", nil))
}
```

Explanation:

The Order Service accepts new orders via HTTP POST, stores them in memory, and asynchronously sends a notification.

3. **Implementing the Inventory Service:** Create a file named inventory_service.go:

```go
go

package main
```

```go
import (
    "encoding/json"
    "log"
    "net/http"
)

type InventoryItem struct {
    Product  string `json:"product"`
    Quantity int    `json:"quantity"`
}

var inventory = []InventoryItem{
    {Product: "Laptop", Quantity: 50},
    {Product: "Smartphone", Quantity: 100},
}

func getInventory(w http.ResponseWriter, r
*http.Request) {
    w.Header().Set("Content-Type",
"application/json")
    json.NewEncoder(w).Encode(inventory)
}

func main() {
    http.HandleFunc("/inventory", getInventory)
    log.Println("Inventory Service running on port
8004...")
    log.Fatal(http.ListenAndServe(":8084", nil))
}
```

Explanation:
The Inventory Service provides a simple endpoint to view product quantities.

4. **API Gateway Implementation:** Create a file named gateway.go that routes requests to the appropriate microservice:

```go
go

package main

import (
    "io"
    "log"
    "net/http"
```

```go
)

func proxyRequest(target string, w
http.ResponseWriter, r *http.Request) {
    resp, err := http.Get(target)
    if err != nil {
        http.Error(w, "Service Unavailable",
http.StatusServiceUnavailable)
        return
    }
    defer resp.Body.Close()
    w.Header().Set("Content-Type",
"application/json")
    io.(w, resp.Body)
}

func main() {
    http.HandleFunc("/orders", func(w
http.ResponseWriter, r *http.Request) {
        proxyRequest("http://localhost:8083/orders",
w, r)
    })
    http.HandleFunc("/inventory", func(w
http.ResponseWriter, r *http.Request) {

proxyRequest("http://localhost:8084/inventory", w, r)
    })
    log.Println("API Gateway running on port
8080...")
    log.Fatal(http.ListenAndServe(":8080", nil))
}
```

Explanation:

The API gateway forwards requests to the Order Service or Inventory Service, providing a unified interface.

5. **Deploying with Concurrency Patterns:** Enhance the Order Service by implementing a worker pool to process orders concurrently. Use a buffered channel and wait groups to manage workers.

```go
go

package main

import (
```

```go
    "encoding/json"
    "log"
    "net/http"
    "sync"
)

type Order struct {
    ID        int     `json:"id"`
    Product   string  `json:"product"`
    Quantity  int     `json:"quantity"`
}

var ordersChan = make(chan Order, 100)
var wg sync.WaitGroup

func worker(id int) {
    defer wg.Done()
    for order := range ordersChan {
        log.Printf("Worker %d processing Order ID
%d", id, order.ID)
        // Simulate processing time
        sendNotification(order)
    }
}

func createOrder(w http.ResponseWriter, r
*http.Request) {
    var order Order
    err := json.NewDecoder(r.Body).Decode(&order)
    if err != nil {
        http.Error(w, "Invalid order data",
http.StatusBadRequest)
        return
    }
    ordersChan <- order
    w.Header().Set("Content-Type",
"application/json")
    json.NewEncoder(w).Encode(order)
}

func sendNotification(order Order) {
    log.Printf("Notification sent for Order ID %d",
order.ID)
}
```

```
func main() {
    // Start worker pool
    numWorkers := 5
    wg.Add(numWorkers)
    for i := 1; i <= numWorkers; i++ {
        go worker(i)
    }
    http.HandleFunc("/orders", createOrder)
    log.Println("Order Service with Worker Pool
running on port 8083...")
    log.Fatal(http.ListenAndServe(":8083", nil))
    close(ordersChan)
    wg.Wait()
}
```

Explanation:
This version of the Order Service processes orders using a worker pool, increasing throughput and resilience under heavy load.

---

5. Advanced Techniques & Optimization

In this section, we explore strategies to further optimize performance, scalability, and concurrency in advanced applications.

5.1 Optimization Strategies

- **Code Refactoring:**
  Continuously refactor your code to eliminate bottlenecks and improve readability.

- **Profiling Revisited:**
  Regularly profile your microservices and network applications to identify performance hotspots.

- **Caching Mechanisms:**
  Implement caching at various layers (e.g., API gateway, microservices) to reduce database load and latency.

- **Database Optimization:**
  Use connection pooling and query optimization techniques for scalable data access.

5.2 Advanced Networking Techniques

- **TLS/SSL Encryption:**
  Secure your network communications by implementing TLS for your TCP servers.

- **Non-Blocking I/O:**
  Use Go's concurrency primitives to perform non-blocking network operations.

- **Custom Protocols:**
  Design custom network protocols when standard ones do not meet your performance needs.

5.3 Advanced Concurrency Patterns

- **Mutexes vs. Channels:**
  Understand the trade-offs between using mutexes for shared state and channels for communication.

- **Context Package:**
  Use the context package to manage cancellation and timeouts across goroutines.

- **Rate Limiting:**
  Implement rate limiting to control resource usage in high-concurrency environments.

- **Load Testing:**
  Use benchmarking and stress testing to simulate real-world loads and identify concurrency issues.

6. Troubleshooting and Problem-Solving

Even advanced systems encounter challenges. This section outlines common pitfalls, troubleshooting strategies, and real-world examples of resolving issues.

6.1 Common Challenges

- **Performance Bottlenecks:**
  Identify slow functions using profiling and optimize them.

- **Race Conditions:**
  Use the -race flag and proper synchronization to avoid data races.

- **Deadlocks:**
  Ensure that all channels are properly closed and that locks are acquired and released in a consistent order.

- **Network Latency:**
  Optimize network code by reducing round trips and using asynchronous processing.

6.2 Debugging Techniques

- **Detailed Logging:**
  Integrate structured logging to capture detailed context when issues arise.

- **Monitoring Dashboards:**
  Use tools like Prometheus and Grafana to monitor real-time metrics.

- **Simulated Testing:**
  Run load tests using tools such as Apache JMeter or Locust to simulate real-world conditions.

- **Code Reviews:**
  Collaborate with peers to review advanced concurrency and network code.

Before-and-After Example:
Show how profiling and logging revealed a deadlock in a worker pool, and then how refactoring the synchronization logic resolved the issue.

---

7. Conclusion & Next Steps

As we conclude this chapter on advanced topics, let's summarize the key points and outline next steps to further deepen your mastery of Go.

Key Takeaways

- **Performance Tuning:**
  Profiling, debugging, and optimizing are essential for creating efficient, scalable applications.

- **Network Programming:**
  Go's robust networking libraries empower you to build both reliable and high-performance networked applications, using TCP/UDP protocols as needed.

- **Advanced Concurrency:**
  Beyond basic goroutines, mastering synchronization techniques and advanced patterns is crucial for leveraging modern multi-core processors.

- **Practical Application:**
  Hands-on projects, from data processing to microservices, illustrate how advanced concepts are applied in real-world scenarios.

- **Continuous Learning:**
  Advanced topics require ongoing refinement, monitoring, and iterative improvements to stay ahead of evolving challenges.

Reflecting on Your Learning

By exploring performance tuning, network programming, and advanced concurrency, you now have a toolkit for optimizing and scaling your applications. These techniques are vital for building systems that perform reliably under high load and in distributed environments.

Next Steps

- **Deepen Your Expertise:**
  Continue exploring advanced Go features, such as more sophisticated synchronization patterns and custom network protocols.

- **Experiment:**
  Apply these techniques to your projects, and integrate monitoring and automated testing to ensure continued performance.

- **Collaborate:**
  Engage with the Go community through forums, meetups, and open-source projects to share experiences and learn from others.

- **Stay Updated:**
  Follow industry trends and updates in Go to continuously refine your skills.

Final Thoughts

Advanced topics are the gateway to building applications that not only work but excel under pressure. Whether you're optimizing a critical system for low latency or architecting a distributed network application, the concepts and techniques covered in this chapter empower you to push the boundaries of what's possible with Go.

By integrating performance tuning, robust network programming, and advanced concurrency into your workflow, you'll be well-prepared to tackle the challenges of modern, high-performance application development. Keep experimenting, keep refining, and let your code evolve with the demands of the real world.

Happy coding, and may your applications run fast, scale smoothly, and handle every challenge with resilience!

Chapter 9: Challenges and Solutions

1. Introduction

In every software project, challenges are inevitable. No matter how well you design your application, issues—from subtle bugs and performance bottlenecks to architectural pitfalls and maintainability concerns—will arise. In Go, as in any programming language, confronting these challenges head-on is essential for developing robust, reliable, and scalable applications.

This chapter focuses on three interrelated areas:

- **Common Pitfalls:** We will discuss real-world challenges encountered by Go developers, including issues related to error handling, concurrency, and resource management, and explore proven solutions.

- **Troubleshooting:** Detailed debugging techniques, error tracing strategies, and methods for improving code reliability will be presented. We'll demonstrate how to diagnose and fix issues using both simple print-debugging and more sophisticated tools.

- **Best Practices:** Finally, we'll cover guidelines for writing clean code, proper documentation, and strategies for maintaining scalability over time. These best practices are key to ensuring that your codebase remains understandable and maintainable as it grows.

Why This Chapter Matters

Facing challenges is a natural part of the software development process. However, the ability to identify and resolve these issues quickly and effectively can make the difference between a project that stalls under technical debt and one that scales gracefully. This chapter is designed to empower you with the knowledge and tools needed to troubleshoot effectively and implement best practices that prevent problems before they occur.

Key Terminology

Before diving deeper, let's define some key terms:

- **Pitfalls:** Common errors or oversights that can lead to bugs or performance issues.

- **Debugging:** The process of finding and resolving defects or problems in your code.

- **Error Tracing:** Techniques used to follow the flow of execution and understand where errors occur.

- **Best Practices:** Standardized methods and guidelines that have been proven to produce high-quality, maintainable code.

- **Scalability:** The capability of a system to handle growth in workload without compromising performance.

Setting the Tone

Throughout this chapter, you'll find real-world examples and hands-on projects that illustrate both the challenges and the solutions. Think of this chapter as a troubleshooting toolkit and style guide all in one. By the end, you'll have a solid understanding of common Go pitfalls, know how to diagnose issues effectively, and be equipped with best practices to maintain and scale your applications over time.

Imagine a seasoned mechanic who not only knows how to fix a car but also how to keep it running efficiently for years. This chapter is your workshop—a place where you learn how to diagnose issues, implement fixes, and adopt strategies that ensure your software remains in top condition.

2. Core Concepts and Theory

In this section, we break down the fundamental principles behind challenges in Go development. We examine common pitfalls, explain key troubleshooting techniques, and explore best practices that form the foundation for writing clean, scalable, and reliable code.

2.1 Common Pitfalls in Go Development

2.1.1 Error Handling Oversights

One of the most common pitfalls in Go is neglecting to check and handle errors properly. Go's explicit error-handling model requires developers to check returned error values. Failing to do so can lead to unexpected behavior or crashes.

Example of a Pitfall:

```go

result, _ := divide(10, 0)
// Ignoring the error may lead to incorrect behavior.
fmt.Println("Result:", result)
Proven Solution:
Always handle errors explicitly:
go

result, err := divide(10, 0)
if err != nil {
    fmt.Println("Error:", err)
    return
}
fmt.Println("Result:", result)
```

2.1.2 Concurrency Issues

Concurrency in Go is powerful, but it comes with its own set of challenges such as race conditions, deadlocks, and goroutine leaks.

Common Pitfall:

- **Race Conditions:** When multiple goroutines access shared data without proper synchronization.

- **Deadlocks:** Occur when goroutines wait indefinitely for each other.

- **Goroutine Leaks:** When goroutines are not properly terminated, causing resource exhaustion.

Proven Solutions:

- Use the -race flag during testing to detect race conditions.

- Employ synchronization primitives like mutexes, channels, or wait groups.

- Always ensure that channels are closed properly and that goroutines have exit conditions.

Example: Using Mutex to Avoid Race Conditions

```go
go

var (
    counter int
    mu      sync.Mutex
)

func safeIncrement() {
    mu.Lock()
    counter++
    mu.Unlock()
}
```

2.1.3 Resource Management and Memory Leaks

Even though Go has garbage collection, improper management of resources (like open files or network connections) can lead to memory leaks or resource exhaustion.

Pitfall Example: Failing to close a file after reading:

```go
go

file, err := os.Open("data.txt")
if err != nil {
    log.Fatal(err)
}
// Missing file.Close() can cause resource leaks.
Proven Solution:
go

file, err := os.Open("data.txt")
if err != nil {
    log.Fatal(err)
```

```
}
defer file.Close()
// Process the file...
```

2.2 Troubleshooting Techniques

Effective troubleshooting involves systematic approaches to diagnosing and fixing problems.

2.2.1 Debugging with Logging

Logging is an invaluable tool for tracing the flow of execution and identifying where errors occur. Use structured logging to provide context.

Example: Structured Logging

```go
log.Printf("Processing user ID %d: starting
operation", userID)
// ... operation ...
log.Printf("Processing user ID %d: completed
operation", userID)
```

2.2.2 Interactive Debugging

Modern IDEs like GoLand or Visual Studio Code offer integrated debugging tools. Setting breakpoints, stepping through code, and inspecting variables are critical to understanding complex issues.

Tip:
Use the built-in debugger to pause execution at suspected problematic areas and inspect state.

2.2.3 Profiling and Performance Tracing

Profiling tools such as Go's pprof help identify performance bottlenecks. Regular profiling is essential to ensure that optimizations are effective.

Example: CPU Profiling with pprof

```go
f, err := os.Create("cpu.prof")
if err != nil {
    log.Fatal(err)
}
```

```go
defer f.Close()
pprof.StartCPUProfile(f)
defer pprof.StopCPUProfile()
```

2.3 Best Practices for Clean Code and Scalability

2.3.1 Clean Code Principles

Writing clean code is crucial for long-term maintainability. Key practices include:

- **Consistent Naming Conventions:** Use clear, descriptive names.

- **Modularity:** Break down your code into reusable functions and packages.

- **Documentation:** Write comments and use tools like GoDoc to generate documentation.

Example: Commenting for Clarity

go

```go
// fetchData retrieves data from the external API and
returns the result.
// It returns an error if the request fails.
func fetchData(url string) ([]byte, error) {
    // Implementation goes here...
}
```

2.3.2 Maintaining Scalability

As your codebase grows, ensuring scalability becomes paramount. Strategies include:

- **Refactoring Regularly:** Continuously improve code structure.

- **Automated Testing:** Use unit and integration tests to catch issues early.

- **CI/CD Pipelines:** Automate testing and deployment to ensure that changes do not break the system.

- **Monitoring:** Implement logging and performance monitoring to quickly identify and address issues.

2.3.3 Documentation and Code Reviews

Thorough documentation and regular code reviews help maintain code quality. Documentation makes it easier for new team members to understand the codebase, while reviews can catch potential issues before they become problems.

Best Practice:
Adopt a culture of peer review where every significant change is reviewed by at least one other developer.

---

3. Tools and Setup

In this section, we detail the tools and platforms required to implement effective troubleshooting, logging, and testing practices in Go. Setting up your environment correctly is the first step toward maintaining high code quality and scalability.

3.1 Essential Tools

- **Go Compiler and Runtime:**
  Download from golang.org/dl.

- **IDE or Text Editor:**
  Visual Studio Code, GoLand, or Sublime Text with Go plugins.

- **Version Control (Git):**
  For managing changes and collaborating with others.

- **Profiling Tools:**
  Go's built-in pprof tool for performance profiling.

- **Logging Libraries:**
  Consider using standard log package or third-party libraries like Logrus or Zap for structured logging.

- **Monitoring Tools:**
  Prometheus and Grafana can be used for monitoring live applications.

- **Debugging Tools:**
  Wireshark for network debugging and integrated IDE debuggers.

3.2 Environment Setup

1. **Workspace Configuration:**

bash

```bash
mkdir -p $HOME/go/{src,pkg,bin}
export GOPATH=$HOME/go
export PATH=$PATH:$GOPATH/bin
source ~/.bashrc
```

2. **IDE Setup:**

   o   Install Visual Studio Code.

   o   Add the Go extension.

   o   Configure debugging settings. *Screenshot Suggestion:* A screenshot showing VS Code with Go code, breakpoints, and log output.

3. **Profiling and Logging Setup:**

   o   Ensure you have tools like pprof installed.

   o   Configure logging libraries if you choose to use alternatives to the standard log package. *Diagram:* A flowchart showing how profiling data flows from your application to a visualization tool.

4. **Version Control:**

   o   Set up Git and link your code repository.

   o   Use branching and pull requests for collaborative code reviews.

---

4. Hands-on Examples & Projects

This section features practical projects that illustrate common challenges and the solutions for them. Each example includes clear, well-documented code, along with diagrams and screenshots suggestions to enhance understanding.

Project 1: Diagnosing and Fixing Concurrency Issues

Overview

In this project, you will simulate a common concurrency problem—a race condition—and then apply debugging techniques and synchronization to resolve it.

Step-by-Step Walkthrough

1. **Simulating a Race Condition:** Create a file named race_condition.go:

```go
package main

import (
    "fmt"
    "sync"
)

var counter int

func increment(wg *sync.WaitGroup) {
    defer wg.Done()
    for i := 0; i < 1000; i++ {
        counter++
    }
}

func main() {
    var wg sync.WaitGroup
    for i := 0; i < 5; i++ {
        wg.Add(1)
        go increment(&wg)
    }
    wg.Wait()
    fmt.Println("Counter:", counter)
}
```

Observation:
Run with go run -race race_condition.go to detect the race condition.

2. **Fixing the Race Condition with Mutex:** Modify the code to use a mutex:

```go
package main

import (
    "fmt"
    "sync"
)

var counter int
var mu sync.Mutex

func increment(wg *sync.WaitGroup) {
    defer wg.Done()
    for i := 0; i < 1000; i++ {
        mu.Lock()
        counter++
        mu.Unlock()
    }
}

func main() {
    var wg sync.WaitGroup
    for i := 0; i < 5; i++ {
        wg.Add(1)
        go increment(&wg)
    }
    wg.Wait()
    fmt.Println("Counter:", counter)
}
```

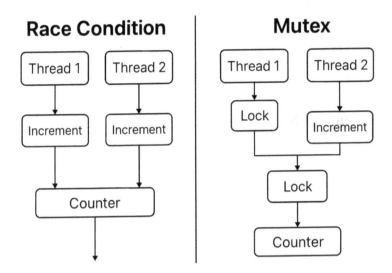

3. **Logging and Debugging:** Add logging statements to trace the execution flow:

```go
func increment(wg *sync.WaitGroup, id int) {
    defer wg.Done()
    for i := 0; i < 1000; i++ {
        mu.Lock()
        counter++
        if counter%500 == 0 {
            fmt.Printf("Worker %d reached %d\n", id,
counter)
        }
        mu.Unlock()
    }
}
```

Explanation:
These log statements help you monitor progress and verify that the synchronization is working correctly.

Project 2: Troubleshooting a Web API

Overview

In this project, you'll build a simple RESTful API with intentional errors, then use debugging and testing tools to identify and fix them. This project simulates real-world issues such as incorrect routing and error handling.

Step-by-Step Walkthrough

1. **Creating a Faulty API:** Create a file named faulty_api.go:

```go
package main

import (
    "encoding/json"
    "fmt"
    "log"
    "net/http"
)

type Item struct {
    ID      int      `json:"id"`
    Name    string  `json:"name"`
}

var items = []Item{
    {ID: 1, Name: "Item One"},
    {ID: 2, Name: "Item Two"},
}

// Incorrectly named handler; routing error.
func getItems(w http.ResponseWriter, r *http.Request)
{
    w.Header().Set("Content-Type",
"application/json")
    json.NewEncoder(w).Encode(items)
}

func main() {
    // Intentionally incorrect URL mapping
    http.HandleFunc("/item", getItems)
    log.Println("Faulty API running on port 8085...")
```

```
    log.Fatal(http.ListenAndServe(":8085", nil))
}
```

Observation:

Notice that the endpoint /item should be /items based on our data.
Additionally, error handling is minimal.

2. **Troubleshooting and Fixing:** Update the code:

```go
package main

import (
    "encoding/json"
    "log"
    "net/http"
)

type Item struct {
    ID      int     `json:"id"`
    Name    string  `json:"name"`
}

var items = []Item{
    {ID: 1, Name: "Item One"},
    {ID: 2, Name: "Item Two"},
}

func getItems(w http.ResponseWriter, r *http.Request) {
    w.Header().Set("Content-Type",
"application/json")
    if err := json.NewEncoder(w).Encode(items); err
!= nil {
        http.Error(w, "Failed to encode items",
http.StatusInternalServerError)
    }
}

func main() {
    // Corrected URL mapping.
    http.HandleFunc("/items", getItems)
    log.Println("API running on port 8085...")
    log.Fatal(http.ListenAndServe(":8085", nil))
```

```
}
```

3. **Testing with Postman:** Use Postman to send requests to http://localhost:8085/items and verify that the JSON output is correct. Document any errors in a testing log.

Project 3: Best Practices for Clean Code in a Microservice

Overview

This project demonstrates best practices by refactoring an existing microservice for improved readability, maintainability, and scalability. You will refactor code, add documentation, and implement unit tests.

Step-by-Step Walkthrough

1. **Initial Code Example:** Create a file named legacy_service.go:

```go
package main

import (
    "encoding/json"
    "net/http"
)

type legacyItem struct {
    Id    int    `json:"id"`
    Name string `json:"name"`
}

var legacyItems = []legacyItem{
    {Id: 1, Name: "Legacy One"},
    {Id: 2, Name: "Legacy Two"},
}

func legacyHandler(w http.ResponseWriter, r
*http.Request) {
    json.NewEncoder(w).Encode(legacyItems)
}
```

```go
func main() {
    http.HandleFunc("/legacy", legacyHandler)
    http.ListenAndServe(":8086", nil)
}
```

Observation:
The code is functional but lacks clear naming, error handling, and documentation.

2. **Refactoring for Best Practices:** Create a file named refactored_service.go:

go

```go
package main

import (
    "encoding/json"
    "log"
    "net/http"
)

// Item represents a product in our legacy service.
type Item struct {
    ID   int    `json:"id"`
    Name string `json:"name"`
}

// items holds the list of legacy items.
var items = []Item{
    {ID: 1, Name: "Legacy One"},
    {ID: 2, Name: "Legacy Two"},
}

// getItemsHandler responds with the list of items in
JSON format.
func getItemsHandler(w http.ResponseWriter, r
*http.Request) {
    w.Header().Set("Content-Type",
"application/json")
    if err := json.NewEncoder(w).Encode(items); err
!= nil {
        http.Error(w, "Failed to encode items",
http.StatusInternalServerError)
        log.Println("Error encoding items:", err)
```

```go
    }
}

func main() {
    http.HandleFunc("/items", getItemsHandler)
    log.Println("Refactored Service running on port 8086...")
    if err := http.ListenAndServe(":8086", nil); err != nil {
        log.Fatal("Server failed:", err)
    }
}
```

Explanation:
This refactored version uses clearer naming conventions, includes error handling, and adds logging for troubleshooting. Documentation comments provide context.

3. **Unit Testing the Service:** Create a file named refactored_service_test.go:

```go
package main

import (
    "encoding/json"
    "net/http"
    "net/http/httptest"
    "testing"
)

func TestGetItemsHandler(t *testing.T) {
    req, err := http.NewRequest("GET", "/items", nil)
    if err != nil {
        t.Fatal(err)
    }

    rr := httptest.NewRecorder()
    handler := http.HandlerFunc(getItemsHandler)

    handler.ServeHTTP(rr, req)

    if status := rr.Code; status != http.StatusOK {
```

```
        t.Errorf("Handler returned wrong status code:
got %v want %v", status, http.StatusOK)
    }

    var gotItems []Item
    if err :=
json.NewDecoder(rr.Body).Decode(&gotItems); err !=
nil {
        t.Errorf("Failed to decode response: %v",
err)
    }
    if len(gotItems) != len(items) {
        t.Errorf("Expected %d items, got %d",
len(items), len(gotItems))
    }
}
```

Explanation:
This test checks that the /items endpoint returns the correct HTTP status
and JSON data. It ensures that the refactored code meets expected
behavior.

---

5. Advanced Techniques & Optimization

As you build more complex systems, refining your troubleshooting and
best practices becomes essential. This section dives deeper into advanced
optimization strategies, including detailed code reviews and refactoring
practices, which help in long-term maintainability.

5.1 Advanced Debugging and Profiling

- **Integrate Structured Logging:**
  Use libraries like Logrus or Zap to produce detailed, structured
  logs that are easier to analyze.

- **Automated Testing and Continuous Integration:**
  Set up CI pipelines to run your tests automatically on every
  commit.

- **Code Reviews:**
  Establish a code review culture. Peer reviews often catch issues that automated tests might miss.

- **Refactoring Workshops:**
  Periodically revisit older code to refactor and improve its structure based on new insights.

5.2 Scalability Best Practices

- **Modularization:**
  Break your code into reusable packages.

- **Documentation:**
  Use clear, concise documentation. Tools like GoDoc help generate documentation from your comments.

- **Consistent Error Handling:**
  Adopt idiomatic error handling practices to ensure that all components handle failures gracefully.

- **Monitoring and Alerting:**
  Use monitoring tools to get real-time feedback on application performance and trigger alerts when issues occur.

5.3 Optimization Trade-offs

Understand the trade-offs between:

- **Performance and Readability:**
  Sometimes highly optimized code can be less readable. Balance performance gains with maintainability.

- **Security vs. Usability:**
  Security measures are essential, but they must not overly burden the user experience.

- **Resource Utilization and Scalability:**
  Optimize for current load while planning for future growth.

6. Troubleshooting and Problem-Solving

Troubleshooting complex applications requires a systematic approach. In this section, we outline strategies and practical examples for diagnosing and fixing issues.

6.1 Common Troubleshooting Challenges

- **Intermittent Bugs:**
  Use detailed logs and run tests under different conditions to reproduce and isolate intermittent issues.

- **Performance Degradation:**
  Profile your code to pinpoint slow functions. Optimize hotspots and refactor inefficient algorithms.

- **Concurrency Issues:**
  Use the -race flag and debugging tools to detect race conditions and deadlocks.

- **Integration Failures:**
  When services communicate over a network, use network tracing and monitoring tools to diagnose failures.

6.2 Step-by-Step Troubleshooting Process

1. **Identify the Problem:**
   Start by reproducing the issue. Use logging and monitoring to gather data.

2. **Isolate the Cause:**
   Break down your application into smaller components. Write tests to isolate the problematic module.

3. **Apply a Fix:**
   Modify the code using best practices (e.g., proper error handling, synchronization).

4. **Test the Solution:**
   Run unit and integration tests. Use profiling tools to confirm that performance issues are resolved.

5. **Document the Fix:**
Update documentation and comments to explain the changes.

Before-and-After Example:
Show how an intermittent race condition was identified using the -race flag
and then resolved with proper locking mechanisms.

6.3 Tools for Effective Troubleshooting

- **Go's Race Detector:**
Use go run -race to find concurrency issues.

- **Profiling Tools (pprof):**
Generate and analyze CPU and memory profiles.

- **IDE Debuggers:**
Use breakpoints and step-through debugging in your IDE.

- **Logging Libraries:**
Structured logging frameworks like Logrus or Zap help capture
detailed error contexts.

- **Monitoring Solutions:**
Integrate Prometheus and Grafana for real-time monitoring of
application metrics.

7. Conclusion & Next Steps

As we conclude this chapter on challenges and solutions, let's recap the
key lessons and outline how you can continue to refine your
troubleshooting and coding practices.

Key Takeaways

- **Anticipate Common Pitfalls:**
Whether it's error handling, concurrency, or resource
management, be proactive in addressing potential issues.

- **Systematic Troubleshooting:**
Use logging, profiling, and structured debugging to identify and
resolve issues efficiently.

- **Adopt Best Practices:**
  Write clean, modular, and well-documented code. Regularly review and refactor your code to maintain scalability.

- **Continuous Monitoring and Testing:**
  Integrate automated tests, continuous integration, and monitoring into your development cycle to catch issues early.

- **Collaboration:**
  Code reviews and team collaboration are critical for uncovering subtle bugs and improving code quality over time.

Reflecting on Your Learning

In this chapter, you've seen that challenges are not roadblocks but opportunities to improve your skills. By understanding common pitfalls, mastering troubleshooting techniques, and adhering to best practices, you can build resilient and scalable applications. Each debugging session, code review, and refactoring effort is a step toward becoming a more proficient and thoughtful developer.

Next Steps

- **Practice Regularly:**
  Apply these strategies in your daily coding projects. The more you practice troubleshooting, the more efficient you'll become.

- **Expand Your Toolkit:**
  Explore advanced debugging tools, contribute to open-source projects, and learn from the broader Go community.

- **Keep Learning:**
  Stay updated with the latest best practices in error handling, performance optimization, and scalable system design.

- **Document Your Journey:**
  Maintain detailed documentation of the challenges you encounter and the solutions you implement. This practice not only benefits your future self but also your team.

Final Thoughts

Every challenge you face in software development is an opportunity to learn and improve. The strategies and best practices discussed in this chapter are not just theoretical—they are practical tools that you can apply to ensure your applications are robust, efficient, and scalable. Whether you're debugging a subtle concurrency issue or optimizing your code for better performance, remember that a systematic, thoughtful approach will always lead to better outcomes.

As you continue on your journey as a Go developer, keep refining your processes, collaborate with your peers, and never shy away from tackling the tough challenges. With persistence, continuous learning, and a focus on best practices, you'll build software that stands the test of time.

Happy coding, and may every challenge be an opportunity to build something even better!

Chapter 10: Final Project – From Concept to Deployment

This chapter brings together everything you've learned so far by guiding you through the complete lifecycle of building a scalable application—from initial concept and planning to coding, testing, deployment, and maintenance. Whether you're a beginner, professional, or hobbyist, this final project integrates core principles, advanced techniques, and best practices to help you create a production-ready system. We'll also discuss potential real-world applications in industries such as manufacturing, healthcare, and logistics.

In this chapter, you will:

- **Project Overview:** Understand the scope and objectives of the final project.

- **Step-by-Step Guide:** Follow detailed instructions on planning, coding, testing, deploying, and maintaining your application.

- **Real-World Applications:** Explore how the techniques and architecture can be applied across various industries.

Throughout the chapter, practical examples, well-commented code snippets, and suggested diagrams will illustrate each step. Let's begin this journey from concept to deployment.

---

1. Introduction

In today's competitive technology landscape, building a complete, scalable application is a vital skill. It's not enough to write code that works in a controlled environment; real-world applications must handle increasing loads, adapt to changing requirements, and remain maintainable over time.

Why You Should Care

Imagine developing an application that grows from a small prototype to a system supporting thousands of users in a dynamic industry like healthcare or manufacturing. The ability to design, build, and deploy such systems ensures your work is both future-proof and robust. This final project not only tests your technical skills but also your ability to integrate various aspects of software development—from architecture to performance optimization.

Key Concepts and Terminology

Before we dive in, let's define some essential terms:

- **Scalable Application:** A system designed to handle growth in users, transactions, or data volume efficiently.

- **Microservices:** A software architecture style in which complex applications are composed of small, independent services.

- **RESTful API:** An interface that uses HTTP methods for CRUD operations in a stateless manner.

- **CI/CD Pipeline:** Continuous Integration and Continuous Deployment tools that automate testing and deployment.

- **Load Balancing:** The process of distributing workloads across multiple computing resources.

- **Monitoring & Logging:** Tools and practices for tracking application performance and troubleshooting issues.

- **Containerization:** Packaging an application and its dependencies into a container for consistency across environments.

Setting the Tone

This chapter is structured to build your final project incrementally. We start with high-level planning and design, then move into setting up your environment and coding the application. After that, we cover testing, deployment, and maintenance. Throughout, real-world analogies and diagrams will help clarify complex ideas. Imagine constructing a building— from architectural blueprints and materials selection to construction, inspection, and final finishing touches. Each phase is crucial, and mastering them all will enable you to create robust, scalable applications.

2. Core Concepts and Theory

This section covers the theory and concepts that will guide your final project. You'll learn how to design an application that is modular, scalable, and maintainable, and we'll discuss why these attributes are critical in real-world deployments.

2.1 Architectural Patterns for Scalability

Microservices Architecture

Modern applications increasingly use microservices to break down functionality into independent services. Each service is responsible for a specific business capability, which means you can scale, deploy, and update them independently.

Real-World Analogy:
Think of a car manufacturer where each department (engine, body, interior) works independently. If one department innovates, it doesn't disrupt the others.

Key Benefits:

- **Isolation:** Faults in one service do not crash the entire system.

- **Scalability:** Services can be scaled individually based on demand.

- **Flexibility:** Different services can be built using the most appropriate technology stack.

RESTful API Design

RESTful APIs provide a standardized way to communicate between services. They are stateless, easy to consume, and leverage HTTP methods to perform operations on resources.

Key Principles:

- **Statelessness:** Each request contains all necessary information.

- **Uniform Interface:** Simplifies communication between clients and servers.

- **Resource Orientation:** URLs represent resources, while HTTP methods (GET, POST, etc.) represent actions.

Modular Coding Practices

Breaking your application into modules improves readability, maintainability, and testability. Each module should have a single responsibility and well-defined interfaces.

Best Practices:

- **Separation of Concerns:** Isolate different aspects of functionality.

- **Loose Coupling:** Minimize dependencies between modules.

- **High Cohesion:** Group related functionality together.

2.2 Designing for Deployment and Maintenance

Planning and Requirements

Before writing any code, plan your project thoroughly. Define requirements, sketch out a high-level architecture, and create a timeline with milestones.

Planning Steps:

- **Define Objectives:** What problem does your application solve?

- **Identify Features:** List the core functionalities and how they interact.

- **Sketch Architecture:** Draw diagrams of service interactions and data flow.

- **Set Milestones:** Break the project into phases: design, development, testing, deployment.

Testing and Quality Assurance

Testing is vital to ensure your application works as intended and scales well. Use both unit tests and integration tests to verify functionality.

Testing Strategies:

- **Unit Testing:** Isolate functions and methods.

- **Integration Testing:** Verify that components work together.

- **Performance Testing:** Simulate real-world load to ensure scalability.

Deployment Strategies

Deploying a scalable application often involves using containerization (e.g., Docker), orchestration (e.g., Kubernetes), and CI/CD pipelines. These practices help maintain consistency across environments and enable smooth rollouts.

Key Concepts:

- **Containerization:** Package your application with its dependencies.

- **Orchestration:** Manage multiple containers for scaling and reliability.

- **CI/CD:** Automate testing and deployment to reduce errors.

2.3 Real-World Applications and Industry Relevance

Let's explore how scalable applications impact different industries:

- **Manufacturing:**
  In manufacturing, scalable applications can manage real-time data from sensors, control robotic assembly lines, and optimize supply chains. A microservices-based system can integrate with IoT devices and process massive amounts of data efficiently.

- **Healthcare:**
  In healthcare, scalability is essential for handling patient data, managing electronic health records (EHRs), and supporting telemedicine platforms. Robust APIs ensure that sensitive data is transmitted securely and reliably.

- **Logistics:**
  Logistics companies rely on scalable applications for tracking shipments, optimizing routes, and managing inventory. Real-time processing and high availability are critical to minimize delays and errors.

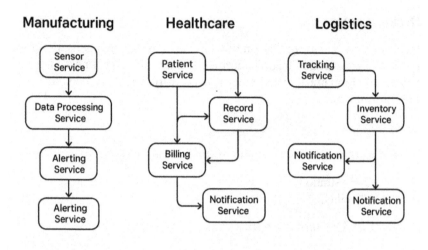

---

3. Tools and Setup

A robust setup is crucial to implement and deploy your final project successfully. This section covers the tools and platforms needed to build, test, and deploy a scalable application.

3.1 Essential Tools and Software

- **Go Compiler and Runtime:**
  Download the latest version from golang.org/dl.

- **IDE or Text Editor:**
  Visual Studio Code, GoLand, or Sublime Text with Go plugins provide powerful code editing and debugging capabilities.

- **Version Control (Git):**
  Git is indispensable for tracking changes and collaborating. Install Git from git-scm.com.

- **Docker:**
  Containerize your application using Docker to ensure consistent environments across development, testing, and production.

- **Kubernetes (Optional):**
  For orchestrating containerized services, consider using Kubernetes.

- **CI/CD Tools:**
  Tools like Jenkins, GitHub Actions, or GitLab CI help automate testing and deployment pipelines.

- **Monitoring and Logging:**
  Integrate Prometheus, Grafana, or ELK stack for performance monitoring and centralized logging.

- **API Testing Tools:**
  Postman or Insomnia are useful for testing RESTful endpoints.

3.2 Setting Up Your Development Environment

Configuring Your Go Workspace

Set up a Go workspace with the following structure:

```bash
mkdir -p $HOME/go/{src,pkg,bin}
export GOPATH=$HOME/go
export PATH=$PATH:$GOPATH/bin
source ~/.bashrc
```

Visual Aid:
A diagram illustrating the Go workspace layout (src, pkg, bin).

IDE and Debugger Setup

Install Visual Studio Code and configure it for Go development:

1. Download VS Code from code.visualstudio.com.

2. Install the Go extension from the Extensions pane.

3. Configure the debugger by setting up launch configurations in VS Code.

Containerization with Docker

To containerize your application:

1. Install Docker from docker.com.

2. Create a Dockerfile in your project directory:

```
dockerfile

FROM golang:1.18-alpine
WORKDIR /app
. .
RUN go build -o final_project .
CMD ["./final_project"]
Build and run your container:
bash

docker build -t final_project .
docker run -p 8080:8080 final_project
```

Diagram Suggestion:
A diagram showing the Docker build process and container deployment.

CI/CD Pipeline Setup

Set up a basic CI/CD pipeline using GitHub Actions:

1. Create a .github/workflows/ci.yml file in your repository.

2. Configure the workflow to run tests and build your application:

```yaml
name: CI
on: [push]
jobs:
  build:
    runs-on: ubuntu-latest
    steps:
      - uses: actions/checkout@v2
      - name: Set up Go
        uses: actions/setup-go@v2
        with:
          go-version: '1.18'
      - name: Build
        run: go build -v ./...
      - name: Test
        run: go test -v ./...
```

4. Hands-on Examples & Projects

This section guides you through the final project—a complete, scalable application built from scratch. The project is divided into several phases: planning, coding, testing, deploying, and maintaining. Each phase is supported by detailed examples, clean code, and diagrams.

Project Overview

Objective:
Build a complete application—a simple order management system—that allows users to create, view, update, and delete orders via a RESTful API. The system will be designed using microservices architecture to ensure scalability and maintainability.

Components:

- **Order Service:** Handles order creation, retrieval, updating, and deletion.

- **API Gateway:** Routes client requests to the appropriate microservice.

- **Database Integration:** Simulate persistent storage using an in-memory database (for simplicity) or a lightweight database like SQLite.

- **Testing Suite:** Comprehensive unit and integration tests to ensure reliability.

- **Deployment Setup:** Containerize the application with Docker and deploy using a CI/CD pipeline.

4.1 Planning Your Application

Requirements Gathering

- **Functional Requirements:**

    o   Create new orders with fields: order ID, customer name, product details, quantity, and status.

    o   Retrieve a list of all orders.

    o   Update order details.

- o   Delete orders.

- **Non-Functional Requirements:**

  - o   Scalability: The system should handle increasing loads.

  - o   Maintainability: Code should be modular and well-documented.

  - o   Performance: Fast response times even under load.

  - o   Security: Input validation and secure error handling.

Architectural Design

Sketch a high-level architecture:

- **Microservices:**
  The Order Service will be a standalone microservice.

- **API Gateway:**
  Acts as the entry point for client requests.

- **Data Layer:**
  A simulated database that stores order information.

Milestones

Divide the project into phases:

1. **Design and Planning:** Define requirements and design architecture.

2. **Development:** Write the code for the Order Service and API Gateway.

3. **Testing:** Develop unit tests and integration tests.

4. **Deployment:** Containerize and deploy the application.

5. **Maintenance:** Set up monitoring and logging.

4.2 Coding the Application
Order Service Implementation

Create a file named order_service.go:

```go
package main

import (
    "encoding/json"
    "log"
    "net/http"
    "strconv"
    "sync"
)

// Order represents an order in the system.
type Order struct {
    ID           int      `json:"id"`
    CustomerName string   `json:"customer_name"`
    Product      string   `json:"product"`
    Quantity     int      `json:"quantity"`
    Status       string   `json:"status"`
}

var (
    orders      = make(map[int]Order)
    orderMutex  sync.Mutex
    nextOrderID = 1
)

// createOrder creates a new order.
func createOrder(w http.ResponseWriter, r
*http.Request) {
    var order Order
    if err := json.NewDecoder(r.Body).Decode(&order);
err != nil {
        http.Error(w, "Invalid order data",
http.StatusBadRequest)
        return
    }
    orderMutex.Lock()
    order.ID = nextOrderID
```

```go
        nextOrderID++
        orders[order.ID] = order
        orderMutex.Unlock()

    w.Header().Set("Content-Type",
"application/json")
        json.NewEncoder(w).Encode(order)
}

// getOrders returns all orders.
func getOrders(w http.ResponseWriter, r
*http.Request) {
        orderMutex.Lock()
        var list []Order
        for _, order := range orders {
            list = append(list, order)
        }
        orderMutex.Unlock()

    w.Header().Set("Content-Type",
"application/json")
        json.NewEncoder(w).Encode(list)
}

// updateOrder updates an existing order.
func updateOrder(w http.ResponseWriter, r
*http.Request) {
        idParam := r.URL.Query().Get("id")
        id, err := strconv.Atoi(idParam)
        if err != nil {
            http.Error(w, "Invalid order ID",
http.StatusBadRequest)
            return
        }

        var updatedOrder Order
        if err :=
json.NewDecoder(r.Body).Decode(&updatedOrder); err !=
nil {
            http.Error(w, "Invalid order data",
http.StatusBadRequest)
            return
        }
```

```go
    orderMutex.Lock()
    order, exists := orders[id]
    if !exists {
        orderMutex.Unlock()
        http.Error(w, "Order not found",
http.StatusNotFound)
        return
    }
    // Update order fields.
    order.CustomerName = updatedOrder.CustomerName
    order.Product = updatedOrder.Product
    order.Quantity = updatedOrder.Quantity
    order.Status = updatedOrder.Status
    orders[id] = order
    orderMutex.Unlock()

    w.Header().Set("Content-Type",
"application/json")
    json.NewEncoder(w).Encode(order)
}

// deleteOrder removes an order.
func deleteOrder(w http.ResponseWriter, r
*http.Request) {
    idParam := r.URL.Query().Get("id")
    id, err := strconv.Atoi(idParam)
    if err != nil {
        http.Error(w, "Invalid order ID",
http.StatusBadRequest)
        return
    }

    orderMutex.Lock()
    _, exists := orders[id]
    if !exists {
        orderMutex.Unlock()
        http.Error(w, "Order not found",
http.StatusNotFound)
        return
    }
    delete(orders, id)
    orderMutex.Unlock()

    w.WriteHeader(http.StatusNoContent)
```

```
}

func main() {
    http.HandleFunc("/orders/create", createOrder)
    http.HandleFunc("/orders", getOrders)
    http.HandleFunc("/orders/update", updateOrder)
    http.HandleFunc("/orders/delete", deleteOrder)
    log.Println("Order Service running on port
8087...")
    log.Fatal(http.ListenAndServe(":8087", nil))
}
```

Explanation:

This Order Service supports creating, retrieving, updating, and deleting orders. It uses a mutex to protect the shared orders map and simulates persistent storage.

API Gateway Implementation

Create a file named api_gateway.go to route requests to the Order Service:

```go
package main

import (
    "io"
    "log"
    "net/http"
)

func proxyRequest(target string, w
http.ResponseWriter, r *http.Request) {
    resp, err := http.Get(target)
    if err != nil {
        http.Error(w, "Service Unavailable",
http.StatusServiceUnavailable)
        return
    }
    defer resp.Body.Close()
    w.Header().Set("Content-Type",
"application/json")
    io.(w, resp.Body)
}
```

```
func main() {
    http.HandleFunc("/orders", func(w
http.ResponseWriter, r *http.Request) {
        // Forward GET requests to the Order Service.
        if r.Method == "GET" {

proxyRequest("http://localhost:8087/orders", w, r)
        }
    })
    log.Println("API Gateway running on port
8080...")
    log.Fatal(http.ListenAndServe(":8080", nil))
}
```

Explanation:
This API Gateway forwards GET requests to the Order Service. For production, you'd add additional routes and error handling.

4.3 Testing Your Application

Implement unit tests to verify your Order Service functionality. Create a file named order_service_test.go:

go

```
package main

import (
    "bytes"
    "encoding/json"
    "net/http"
    "net/http/httptest"
    "strconv"
    "testing"
)

func TestCreateOrder(t *testing.T) {
    order := Order{CustomerName: "Test Customer",
Product: "Test Product", Quantity: 2, Status: "New"}
    jsonData, _ := json.Marshal(order)
    req, err := http.NewRequest("POST",
"/orders/create", bytes.NewBuffer(jsonData))
    if err != nil {
        t.Fatal(err)
    }
```

```go
    rr := httptest.NewRecorder()
    handler := http.HandlerFunc(createOrder)
    handler.ServeHTTP(rr, req)

    if status := rr.Code; status != http.StatusOK {
        t.Errorf("Expected status code %v, got %v",
http.StatusOK, status)
    }

    var createdOrder Order
    if err :=
json.NewDecoder(rr.Body).Decode(&createdOrder); err
!= nil {
        t.Errorf("Error decoding response: %v", err)
    }
    if createdOrder.CustomerName !=
order.CustomerName {
        t.Errorf("Expected customer name %s, got %s",
order.CustomerName, createdOrder.CustomerName)
    }
}

func TestDeleteOrder(t *testing.T) {
    // First, create an order.
    order := Order{CustomerName: "Delete Test",
Product: "Test Product", Quantity: 1, Status: "New"}
    orderMutex.Lock()
    order.ID = nextOrderID
    nextOrderID++
    orders[order.ID] = order
    orderMutex.Unlock()

    // Now, delete the order.
    req, err := http.NewRequest("DELETE",
"/orders/delete?id="+strconv.Itoa(order.ID), nil)
    if err != nil {
        t.Fatal(err)
    }
    rr := httptest.NewRecorder()
    handler := http.HandlerFunc(deleteOrder)
    handler.ServeHTTP(rr, req)

    if status := rr.Code; status !=
http.StatusNoContent {
```

```
        t.Errorf("Expected status code %v, got %v",
http.StatusNoContent, status)
    }
}
```

Explanation:
These tests verify that order creation and deletion behave as expected.

4.4 Deployment and Maintenance

Containerizing Your Application

Create a Dockerfile for the Order Service:

```
dockerfile

FROM golang:1.18-alpine
WORKDIR /app
. .
RUN go build -o order_service .
CMD ["./order_service"]
```
Build and run your container:

```
bash

docker build -t order_service .
docker run -p 8087:8087 order_service
```

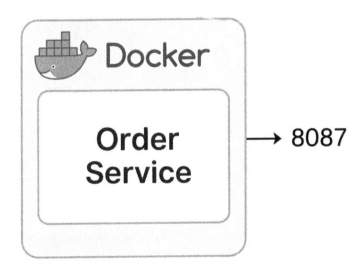

Setting Up a CI/CD Pipeline

Use GitHub Actions or another CI/CD tool to automate testing and deployment. An example workflow (.github/workflows/ci.yml):

```yaml
name: CI/CD Pipeline
on: [push]
jobs:
  build:
    runs-on: ubuntu-latest
    steps:
        - uses: actions/checkout@v2
        - name: Set up Go
          uses: actions/setup-go@v2
          with:
            go-version: '1.18'
        - name: Build Application
          run: go build -v ./...
        - name: Run Tests
          run: go test -v ./...
        - name: Build Docker Image
          run: docker build -t order_service .
        - name: Push Docker Image
          run: echo "Push image to registry (not
implemented)"
```

Maintenance Strategies

- **Monitoring:**
  Use Prometheus and Grafana to monitor performance and error rates.

- **Logging:**
  Centralize logs with tools like ELK or Fluentd.

- **Regular Refactoring:**
  Schedule periodic code reviews and refactoring sessions to maintain code quality.

- **Automated Backups:**
  Implement automated backups for your database and configuration files.

5. Advanced Techniques & Optimization

As your project matures, you'll need to optimize performance and scalability. Advanced techniques include:

- **Performance Tuning:**
  Profile your application regularly and optimize bottlenecks.

- **Load Testing:**
  Use tools like Apache JMeter or Locust to simulate high loads.

- **Advanced Caching Strategies:**
  Implement caching at the API gateway or within microservices.

- **Security Enhancements:**
  Harden your application against common vulnerabilities through input validation, proper error handling, and encryption.

6. Troubleshooting and Problem-Solving

Even after deployment, issues can arise. Follow a systematic approach to troubleshooting:

6.1 Diagnosing Common Issues

- **Intermittent Failures:**
  Use detailed logging and run tests under load.

- **Performance Degradation:**
  Profile your application to identify slow functions.

- **Integration Failures:**
  Check network configurations and ensure that microservices can communicate.

- **Resource Leaks:**
  Monitor resource usage and ensure proper cleanup of resources.

6.2 Step-by-Step Troubleshooting Process

1. **Reproduce the Issue:**
   Use logging and testing tools to replicate the problem.

2. **Isolate the Problem:**
   Narrow down the issue by testing individual components.

3. **Apply Fixes:**
   Implement changes and test their impact.

4. **Document and Monitor:**
   Record the changes and continue to monitor for regressions.

Before-and-After Example:
Show how adding mutex locks eliminated a race condition, with profiling data before and after the change.

6.3 Tools and Techniques for Effective Troubleshooting

- **Race Detector:**
  Run with go run -race to catch concurrency issues.

- **Profiling (pprof):**
  Analyze CPU and memory usage.

- **IDE Debuggers:**
  Set breakpoints and inspect variables in real time.

- **Centralized Logging:**
  Use structured logging to aggregate error data.

---

7. Conclusion & Next Steps

Summary

In this final chapter, you've taken your skills from concept to deployment. You built a complete, scalable application—a fully functional order management system—using microservices, RESTful APIs, and modern development practices. You planned your project meticulously, implemented key features in a modular way, tested rigorously, and deployed the application using containerization and CI/CD pipelines.

What You've Learned

- **End-to-End Development:**
  You learned how to move from initial concept and planning to coding, testing, deployment, and maintenance.

- **Scalability and Modularity:**
  The microservices architecture and RESTful API design allow your application to scale efficiently.

- **Testing and Quality Assurance:**
  Comprehensive unit and integration tests ensure reliability and facilitate continuous improvement.

- **Deployment Best Practices:**
  Containerization and automated CI/CD pipelines streamline deployment and maintenance.

- **Real-World Applications:**
  We discussed how similar architectures can be applied in industries such as manufacturing, healthcare, and logistics.

Next Steps

- **Expand Your Application:**
  Add new features like user authentication, payment processing, or real-time notifications.

- **Integrate with External Services:**
  Connect your microservices to external databases or third-party APIs.

- **Deploy in a Cloud Environment:**
  Use Kubernetes or another orchestration tool to manage your containers in production.

- **Enhance Security:**
  Implement robust security measures such as TLS, OAuth, and regular vulnerability scanning.

- **Monitor and Optimize:**
  Set up continuous monitoring and performance tuning to keep your application running smoothly.

Final Thoughts

Building a scalable application from scratch is a challenging but rewarding endeavor. By following this project—from concept through deployment—you have acquired a comprehensive skill set that prepares you to tackle real-world problems. Every challenge you overcome, every bug you fix, and every optimization you implement is a stepping stone toward becoming a proficient, forward-thinking developer.

Remember, the journey of software development is iterative. Continuous improvement, learning, and collaboration are key to long-term success. Use this final project as a foundation upon which you can build more sophisticated systems, adapt to evolving requirements, and drive innovation in your industry.

Happy coding, and may your future projects be as robust, scalable, and successful as the application you built in this final project!

Chapter 11: Conclusion and Next Steps

In this final chapter, we reflect on your journey through mastering Go and building scalable applications. Here, we consolidate the key concepts, review best practices, and outline actionable steps and resources to propel your learning forward. Whether you're a beginner who has just completed your first project, a professional seeking to deepen your expertise, or a hobbyist excited by the endless possibilities of Go, this chapter is your launchpad for continued innovation and success.

---

1. Introduction

Software development is a journey of continuous learning and improvement. Throughout this book, we've explored Go's core features—from its elegant syntax and powerful concurrency to building real-world scalable applications. In this concluding chapter, we will recap the essential takeaways, provide further learning resources, and offer encouragement to help you keep pushing boundaries.

Why This Chapter Matters

As you close this book, it's important to consolidate what you've learned. Reflection reinforces your knowledge, while looking ahead sparks ideas for future projects. By revisiting the key concepts and outlining next steps, you set the stage for future success. This chapter is not just a summary—it's a roadmap that guides you toward mastering advanced topics, adopting best practices, and engaging with a vibrant community of Go developers.

Key Concepts and Terminology

Before we dive deeper, let's define a few key terms:

- **Recap:** A brief summary of what has been covered.

- **Best Practices:** Proven strategies for writing clean, maintainable, and scalable code.

- **Further Learning:** Resources such as books, online courses, communities, and conferences that can accelerate your continued growth.

- **Next Steps:** Practical actions you can take to apply your knowledge, from starting new projects to joining collaborative groups.

- **Scalability:** The ability of an application to handle increased loads gracefully.

- **Innovation:** Applying creative solutions to solve complex problems.

Setting the Tone

Consider this chapter as your "next chapter" in the broader narrative of your coding journey. As with any journey, the end of one path is the beginning of another. We will revisit the core theories and techniques that have been central to building modern scalable applications in Go. In doing so, you'll not only reinforce your foundation but also gain clarity on how to tackle more advanced challenges in the future.

Imagine you've built a sturdy ship capable of navigating turbulent seas. Now, as you stand on the dock looking back at the long voyage you've undertaken—from learning syntax and fundamentals to deploying microservices—you are poised to sail toward new horizons. This chapter is your captain's log, summarizing your journey and charting your course for future adventures.

2. Core Concepts and Theory

In this section, we review and reinforce the core concepts that have formed the backbone of our exploration of Go. We revisit the key ideas and illustrate how these principles not only helped you build applications but also empower you to think critically about solving real-world problems.

2.1 Recap of Go Fundamentals

Simplicity and Efficiency

Go was designed with simplicity in mind. Its minimalistic syntax and powerful standard library allow you to write code that is both readable and efficient. You learned how:

- **Variables and Data Types:** Provide a strong foundation for managing data.

- **Control Structures and Functions:** Enable modular programming and clean code organization.

- **Pointers and Memory Management:** Give you the power to optimize performance while maintaining safety.

Real-World Analogy:
Think of Go as a well-engineered tool. Just as a high-quality, straightforward tool makes a craftsman's job easier, Go's clarity and efficiency empower you to build robust applications with less friction.

Concurrency

Concurrency is at the heart of Go's design. You discovered how goroutines and channels make it possible to perform multiple tasks concurrently, enabling your applications to scale. Key lessons included:

- **Goroutines:** How to launch lightweight threads with the go keyword.

- **Channels:** How to communicate safely between goroutines.

- **Advanced Patterns:** Worker pools, fan-out/fan-in, and synchronization techniques that prevent race conditions.

Real-World Analogy:
Imagine a busy restaurant where many chefs work together to prepare a meal simultaneously. Just as effective communication and coordination in the kitchen lead to a delicious meal, effective concurrency leads to responsive and scalable applications.

2.2 Recap of Architectural Patterns

Throughout the book, we explored different architectural patterns, including:

- **Microservices:** Breaking an application into independent, loosely coupled services to improve scalability and resilience.

- **RESTful API Design:** Creating standardized interfaces for communication between services.

- **Modular Coding Practices:** Ensuring that your code remains maintainable and adaptable as your project evolves.

Real-World Application:
From e-commerce platforms to healthcare management systems, these architectural principles ensure that applications can handle real-world demands such as fluctuating traffic and evolving business needs.

2.3 Recap of Testing and Error Handling

Testing and error handling are critical to building reliable applications. You learned that:

- **Error Handling:** In Go is explicit and requires you to check error return values, which leads to more robust and predictable code.

- **Unit Testing:** Helps you verify the correctness of individual functions.

- **Integration Testing:** Ensures that different parts of your application work together as expected.

- **Benchmarking:** Allows you to measure performance and optimize where necessary.

Real-World Analogy:
Think of testing as the safety checks performed on a vehicle before a long journey. Just as thorough inspections help prevent breakdowns on the road, rigorous testing helps catch bugs before they impact users.

2.4 Best Practices and Clean Code Principles

To ensure long-term success, adhering to best practices is vital. These include:

- **Consistent Coding Style:** Write clean, consistent code that is easy to read and understand.

- **Documentation:** Keep your code well-documented to ease future maintenance and collaboration.

- **Code Reviews:** Collaborate with peers to catch issues early and share knowledge.

- **Continuous Refactoring:** Regularly improve your codebase to eliminate technical debt.

Real-World Analogy:
Maintaining clean code is like regularly servicing a car. It ensures that the vehicle runs smoothly over time and prevents small issues from developing into major problems.

3. Tools and Setup

This section revisits the essential tools and platforms that have supported your learning and project development. A solid setup is the cornerstone of efficient development, testing, and deployment.

3.1 Essential Software and Platforms

To work effectively with Go, you have used and configured several key tools:

- **Go Compiler and Runtime:**
  The foundation of your development environment, available from golang.org/dl.

- **IDE/Text Editor:**
  Visual Studio Code, GoLand, or Sublime Text—each configured with Go plugins for syntax highlighting, code completion, and debugging.

- **Version Control:**
  Git is used for source code management and collaboration.

- **Containerization Tools:**
  Docker has enabled you to package your applications consistently across different environments.

- **CI/CD Tools:**
  Automated pipelines (e.g., GitHub Actions, Jenkins) have streamlined testing and deployment.

- **Monitoring and Logging:**
  Tools like Prometheus, Grafana, and ELK help ensure that your applications run smoothly in production.

3.2 Environment Setup Recap

Here's a quick refresher on setting up your Go workspace:

1. **Create Your Workspace:**

```bash
```

```
mkdir -p $HOME/go/{src,pkg,bin}
export GOPATH=$HOME/go
export PATH=$PATH:$GOPATH/bin
source ~/.bashrc
```

2. **IDE Configuration:**
   Install Visual Studio Code, add the Go extension, and configure debugging settings.

3. **Version Control Setup:**
   Configure Git with your user details and set up your repository.

4. **Containerization:**
   Install Docker and write Dockerfiles to containerize your applications.

3.3 Additional Tools for Continuous Learning

Beyond the basics, consider integrating these tools for long-term success:

- **Static Analysis Tools:**
  Tools like golint and go vet help maintain code quality.

- **Performance Profilers:**
  Use pprof to continuously monitor and optimize performance.

- **Security Scanners:**
  Integrate security analysis tools to identify and patch vulnerabilities early.

4. Hands-on Examples & Projects Recap

Over the course of this book, you have built several practical projects that illustrate the real-world application of Go's features. Let's briefly revisit these projects and what they taught you.

4.1 Command-Line Tool

You built a CLI tool that manages a to-do list:

- **Key Learnings:**
  Parsing command-line arguments, handling user input, and maintaining state.

- **Practical Outcome:**
  A functional CLI application that demonstrates error handling and input validation.

Visual Aid:
A flowchart showing the user's journey through the CLI tool—from entering a command to seeing the result.

4.2 Web Server Development

You developed a web server using the net/http package:

- **Key Learnings:**
  Routing, handling HTTP requests, JSON encoding/decoding, and middleware for logging.

- **Practical Outcome:**
  A simple web API that serves JSON responses, demonstrating how to build scalable web applications in Go.

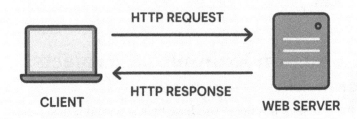

HTTP Request-Response Cycle

HTTP REQUEST

HTTP RESPONSE

CLIENT

WEB SERVER

4.3 Microservices Architecture

Your projects also included building microservices and deploying them behind an API gateway:

- **Key Learnings:**
  Microservices design, inter-service communication via RESTful APIs, and containerization with Docker.

- **Practical Outcome:**
  A scalable, modular system that can be deployed and managed independently.

4.4 Performance Tuning and Advanced Concurrency

Advanced projects introduced you to profiling, debugging, and optimizing code:

- **Key Learnings:**
  Using pprof, debugging with race detectors, and applying advanced concurrency patterns.

- **Practical Outcome:**
  Optimized code that runs efficiently under load, with effective use of Go's concurrency features.

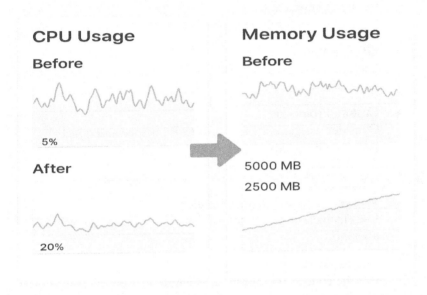

5. Advanced Techniques & Optimization Recap

Before wrapping up, let's review some advanced techniques that you can continue to apply as you further develop your skills.

5.1 Performance Optimization

- **Profiling:**
  Regularly profile your application to catch performance bottlenecks.

- **Optimizing Algorithms:**
  Refactor code to use efficient data structures and minimize resource usage.

- **Benchmarking:**
  Write benchmark tests to measure improvements over time.

5.2 Network Programming Enhancements

- **Secure Communication:**
  Implement TLS/SSL to secure your network communications.

- **Efficient Protocols:**
  Understand when to use TCP versus UDP, and optimize accordingly.

- **Custom Protocols:**
  Consider designing custom protocols for specialized high-performance needs.

5.3 Advanced Concurrency Patterns

- **Worker Pools and Synchronization:**
  Use channels and mutexes wisely to manage concurrent operations.

- **Context Management:**
  Use the context package to handle timeouts and cancellations.

- **Rate Limiting and Backpressure:**
  Implement strategies to prevent system overload in high-concurrency scenarios.

6. Troubleshooting and Problem-Solving Recap

Effective troubleshooting is an essential skill. Here are the key strategies you should always remember:

- **Reproduce the Issue:**
  Use logging and testing to capture the problem.

- **Isolate the Problem:**
  Break down your code into smaller components to pinpoint where the issue lies.

- **Apply Fixes and Verify:**
  Use tests and profiling to ensure that your changes have the desired effect.

- **Document and Learn:**
  Keep records of what went wrong and how you fixed it, so you can avoid similar issues in the future.

Visual Aid:
A troubleshooting flowchart that outlines the process from problem identification to resolution.

7. Conclusion & Next Steps

Recap of Key Takeaways

Throughout this book, you've learned that Go is not only a language built for efficiency and simplicity but also a powerful tool for building scalable, robust, and maintainable applications. Let's summarize the core lessons:

- **Simplicity and Clarity:**
  Go's minimalistic design encourages you to write clean, readable code.

- **Concurrency:**
  Goroutines and channels allow you to handle complex, parallel tasks with ease.

- **Modular Architecture:**
  Building applications with microservices and RESTful APIs makes them more scalable and adaptable.

- **Testing and Error Handling:**
  Rigorous testing and explicit error management are key to creating reliable software.

- **Performance Tuning:**
  Profiling, debugging, and optimization strategies ensure your applications run efficiently even as they scale.

- **Best Practices:**
  Clean code principles, continuous refactoring, and proper
  documentation are the foundations of long-term success.

Further Learning

Your journey doesn't end here. There are numerous resources and
communities that can help you continue growing as a Go developer:

- **Books:**
  - *The Go Programming Language* by Alan A. A. Donovan
    and Brian W. Kernighan

  - *Concurrency in Go* by Katherine Cox-Buday

  - *Building Microservices* by Sam Newman

- **Online Courses:**
  Platforms like Coursera, Pluralsight, and Udacity offer advanced
  courses on Go, microservices, and scalable architectures.

- **Communities:**
  Join online communities such as r/golang, the Go Forum, and
  Slack channels dedicated to Go development.

- **Conferences and Meetups:**
  Attend events like GopherCon, local Go meetups, or virtual
  conferences to network and learn from industry experts.

- **Blogs and Tutorials:**
  Follow the official Go blog, CNCF resources, and other
  technology blogs that provide up-to-date information on best
  practices and new developments.

Encouragement and Reflection

Remember that every project you build is a stepping stone on your journey
to mastery. The challenges you faced and the solutions you implemented
have prepared you for even greater challenges ahead. Your ability to learn
from mistakes, optimize performance, and continuously refine your
approach is what sets you apart as a developer.

Take a moment to reflect on how far you've come—from writing simple "Hello, World!" programs to architecting and deploying scalable, production-ready applications. The skills you've developed here are invaluable. They not only empower you to build robust systems but also to innovate and solve complex problems in any industry you choose.

As you continue to build, experiment, and refine your craft, remember: you can do it. Every bug you fix, every optimization you apply, and every new concept you master is a testament to your growth. Embrace challenges as opportunities to learn, and don't hesitate to push the boundaries of what you can achieve.

Next Steps for Your Journey

- **Start a New Project:**
  Apply your knowledge by starting a new project that excites you. Whether it's a web application, a CLI tool, or a microservice-based system, put your skills to the test.

- **Contribute to Open Source:**
  Join open-source projects to collaborate with other developers, learn new techniques, and share your expertise.

- **Document Your Work:**
  Keep a blog or portfolio of your projects. Not only does this help solidify your knowledge, but it also showcases your skills to potential employers or collaborators.

- **Engage with the Community:**
  Participate in forums, attend meetups, and contribute to discussions. The Go community is vibrant and supportive—learning from others and sharing your own experiences is a great way to grow.

- **Stay Curious:**
  Technologies and best practices evolve. Continue reading, experimenting, and updating your skills to stay ahead of the curve.

Final Thoughts

In the world of software development, the journey is as important as the destination. Every line of code, every challenge overcome, and every new skill acquired contributes to your growth as a developer. Go has provided you with the tools to build efficient, scalable, and robust applications. Now, armed with this knowledge, you are ready to embark on new projects, innovate, and make a lasting impact in the field of software development.

Remember: innovation is a continuous process. The skills you've learned here are just the beginning. With dedication, persistence, and a commitment to quality, you can build systems that not only meet today's challenges but also anticipate tomorrow's needs.

As you move forward, embrace every challenge as a chance to learn and improve. Let the lessons in this book inspire you to push the boundaries of what you can achieve. Your journey as a Go developer is ongoing, and the future is yours to shape.

Happy coding, and here's to your next great project!

www.ingramcontent.com/pod-product-compliance
Lightning Source LLC
Chambersburg PA
CBHW071239050326
40690CB00011B/2182